# SHIVRAJ SINGH
## And Rise Of Madhya Pradesh

# SHIVRAJ SINGH
## AND RISE OF MADHYA PRADESH

Abhilash Khandekar

Vitasta
*Let Knowledge Spread*

Published by
Renu Kaul Verma
Vitasta Publishing Pvt. Ltd.
2/15, Ansari Road, Daryaganj,
New Delhi - 110 002
info@vitastapublishing.com

ISBN 978-93-82711-35-3
© Abhilash Khandekar, 2014
Revised Edition, 2015

All Rights Reserved.
No part of this publication may be reproduced, stored in a retrieval system, or transmitted, in any form, or by any means—electronic, mechanical, photocopying, recording or otherwise—without the prior permission of the publisher.

The views and opinions expressed in this book are the author's own. He is solely responsible for the facts and authenticity of the quotes and sources used for this work. The publisher in no way is liable for the same.

Cover and Layout Design by Vitasta Publishing Pvt. Ltd.
Printed by Vikas Computer and Printers, New Delhi

*To*

Nana and Aai...my parents who
are not in this world but their
blessings made this book possible

# CONTENT

ACKNOWLEDGEMENT ........................................ ix
PREFACE ...................................................... xiii
PROLOGUE .................................................... xxi
INTRODUCTION ............................................ xxvii

| | |
|---|---|
| 1. The Making of Shivraj Jait To Jail | 1 |
| 2. Shivraj, The Politician | 11 |
| 3. The Uma Bharti Factor | 23 |
| 4. Treading Cautiously | 37 |
| 5. Governance | 59 |
| 6. Agrarian Miracle | 71 |
| 7. Social Concerns | 89 |
| 8. The Sports Buff | 95 |
| 9. Bureaucracy, Crime and Corruption | 107 |
| 10. Banishing The BIMARU | 123 |
| 11. Darkness At Noon | 143 |
| 12. BJP: Winning Strokes | 161 |
| Epilogue | 181 |
| Reference | 185 |
| Index | 189 |

# ACKNOWLEDGEMENT

I am actually floundering for the proper words to adequately thank my Editor, Veena Batra who discussed endlessly with me the manuscript, the subject matter and issues that I have tackled in this biographical sketch of Shivraj Singh Chouhan and the contemporary politics of MP. But for her experience, hard work and constant guidance, the book in your hands would not have been what it is.

I had shared the idea of a book first with veteran journalist, political analyst and my professional friend, Girija Shankar, sometime in mid 2013 and later with Manoj Shrivastava, IAS, CM's Principal Secretary and my personal friend for over two decades. It was on Diwali 2013 that Shrivastava broached the subject again and pepped me up. Manoj helped me understand better the unique panchayat concept of the Chief Minister that helped bridge the gap between the government and the people. Both cooperated with me with lots of inputs and ideas.

SK Mishra, IAS, CM's another Principal Secretary, did whatever he could to steal valuable time from his busy boss for my conversations with him—at home, in cars and in his aircraft during his pre-Lok Sabha campaign tours. Rakesh Shrivastava, IAS, Commissioner (Public Relations) and Arun Kumar Bhatt, IAS, Managing Director, MPSIDC, made available innumerable data and decisions of the government; CM's speeches and such other vital inputs with extraordinary speed, even as I was racing against time. I don't have enough words to thank you Mishraji, Rakesh and Arun.

I thank BJP President Narendra Singh Tomar, Indore's Member

of Parliament Sumitra Mahajan, Finance Minister Jayant Malaiya, Energy Minister Rajendra Shukla, Home Minister Babulal Gaur, Member of Parliament (RS) and BJP strategist Anil Dave, party's former spokesman and my childhood friend from Indore Govind Maloo and a large number of BJP workers, MLAs and bureaucrats who gave their own perceptions of the man called Shivraj Singh Chouhan and many other valuable inputs.

Also Dr Padmakar Tripathi, my dear family friend, then Nitin Nandgaonkar and Vikas Dube who all studied with Shivraj Singh at one time or the other and shared their school/college days' memorable moments with me and helped shape the book.

Chandrakant Naidu, my former boss at the *Free Press Journal*, saw the raw copies and made many changes, like he used to do in our newspaper days and helped improve the content. Despite his brief illness, he kept helping me for this book to meet the deadline. A big thank you, Sir.

Virendra Pandit, Bureau Chief of *Business Line* (a Hindu Group of Newspapers' business daily at Ahmedabad), and the author of a beautiful book, *The Biology of History*, was my constant torchbearer. He shared his own experiences and travails of book writing and kept guiding me from his rich personal experience, from day one.

And yes, how can I forget Sunita Aron, Resident Editor of *Hindustan Times* at Lucknow. Her book on Akhilesh Yadav, Chief Minister of Uttar Pradesh, was among my inspirations for writing a book on Shivraj Singh Chouhan. Sunita, thanks for introducing me to Renu Kaul Verma of Vitasta Publishing House, Delhi. Your occasional queries about my writing speed indeed encouraged me to burn more midnight oil and complete the book before the demanding deadline.

Renu was quick to respond and was very upbeat at the suggestion of a book on 'contemporary politics of MP and Shivraj Singh Chouhan'.

Thanks is a small word, Renu!

I must profusely express my gratefulness to the Managing Director, Sudhir Agarwal, of the Dainik Bhaskar Group, for allowing me time to write this book.

My Executive Assistant Vijay Kurkure helped me day and night with my computer issues; he was also a good research assistant.

And last but not the least my wife Anjali, who kept inquiring about the problems that I faced on the way to completing the project, its speed and progress to meet the deadline set by my publishers. She kept me largely free from domestic chores. She did not bother me on Sundays also when I would remain busy in my study—reading, writing and rewriting the chapters of my first book on politics. She helped me in getting precisely the right book or a clipping, from my vast personal reference material collected over the years.

Since I have been working as a journalist in various capacities in Madhya Pradesh for a sufficiently large part of my career, I thought it was easy to write such a book, but delving deep into history to check and counter check facts and figures was not as easy a task as I had thought.

Yet, it was a joy working on this book and I must express my sincere gratefulness to Chief Minister Shivraj Singh who, after initial reluctance, permitted me to go ahead and did spend time with me to share his vision, his background, his future plans and important events in his political career. After his big victory in the Assembly elections, I thought he would have more leisure time at his disposal but that was not to be. He became much busier all over again—a workaholic that he is.

I am indeed grateful to you all.

ଓଓଓ

# PREFACE

I would like to sincerely express my gratitude towards all my readers who liked and patronised this book resulting in a quick demand for the second edition of the same.

Between April 2014, when the first edition hit the market, and now, when the second edition is in your hands, many important political developments took place at the national and state level requiring their inclusion in this book in order to update the readers. The most important among them is the taking over of Narendra Modi as the Prime Minister in May end, 2014. The other happening is of Madhya Pradesh wherein a medical entrance exam and government recruitment scam jolted Shivraj Singh as never before and tarnished his political image to a great extent.

Narendra Modi won with an overwhelming majority and even succeeded in getting his own party—the Bharatiya Janata Party—a massive majority with 282 seats (NDA won 336). This happened for the first time that the BJP, sans veteran founder like LK Advani and MM Joshi, made its presence felt across India since it birth in 1980. 'NaMo' not only pushed Congress to history's lowest score of 44 seats in the Lok Sabha, he began his innings in style by inviting all SAARC countries' Heads of State for his glittering oath-taking ceremony which included Pakistan's Nawaz Sharif too. The new PM got down to work immediately and the message spread faster than it was expected in Delhi and to every nook and corner of the country that he wanted two-three clear things from his team of ministers and bureaucrats: efficiency, transparency and accountability. In other words, he wanted speedy disposal of files and a strict no-no to corruption. He raised hope of good governance and of course, *the Acche din*, as promised by the BJP in his high-voltage electoral campaign.

This had an immediate effect. His ministers started sitting for longer hours in their ministries in Delhi. The PM himself started working from 7am, after doing his yoga and reading etc. He has already made a few trips abroad (Bhutan, Nepal and Japan) and more are planned. No surprise then that the BJP's regional satraps got a message that was very loud and clear—work is worship. Clean, responsive governance with innovation top the agenda of the new PM. The Gujarat model was quite visible in Delhi from the day one. While on the one hand MP's tried and tested pro-people policies were being taken note of by the Centre and other states in some format or the other, Shivraj had another reason to smile, being a performer Chief Minister.

According to the latest figures of GSDP, released by the Central Statistics Office of the Planning Commission, Madhya Pradesh topped the table of growth across Indian states.

*Indian Express* reported on 8 September, 2014, that in the tally of three years showing growth of States GSDP, MP clocked an aggregate of 10.22% with FY 2013-2014 showing India's best growth figures of 11.8% pipping Bihar, Jharkhand, West Bengal, Punjab and Tamil Nadu. Bihar's three aggregate, however, stood a notch above MP at 11.15%.

MP consistently bettered its performance from 9.69% to 9.89% to 11.08 % in three years, mainly due to agricultural growth and expansion of service sector. About agriculture miracles, I have already written inside.

Significantly, this eye-catching growth was registered by Madhya Pradesh at a time when the all-India's GDP was 4.86% in the corresponding year of 2013-2014.

But MP Chief Minister Shivraj Singh Chouhan, who has enjoyed the reputation of being a good administrator with a clean image, got entangled in a huge admission and recruitments scam involving a government organisation 'Vyapam' (the Professional Exams Board). Although no charge stuck on him personally, the opposition Congress' manifold attacks on him and his government, besides family members, including wife Sadhana, weakened him a bit.

Hundreds and thousands of exams were conducted by this organisation which was once headed by an Additional Chief Secretary rank's IAS officer. However, what turned out to be a systematic scam was that those who had right contacts at the right place, got into medical colleges and/or pocketed government jobs of police constable, forest guard or employment assistant and such other posts, passing the exams through dubious means rather than on merit. The scam was reportedly going on for a few years without any cognisance being taken by the government, nay Shivraj. His government's important minister and the CM's one-time close colleague, Laxmi Kant Sharma, holding technical education portfolio for full five years from 2008-2013, turned out to be the kingpin of the scam. State police's intelligence department or the CM's own channels of communication, if any he had, let him down completely. Sharma was not only close to the CM but also to the RSS. Its leader Suresh Soni, often charged with allegations in hush-hush tones in the media and political circles, unlike his peers in the RSS—most of whom are considered above board— was also dragged into the controversy, besides the late KC Sudarshan, former Sarasanghchalak (the top boss) of the RSS. This actually angered the RSS no end.

While Shivraj stoutly defended himself against the attacks, he was much distressed and disturbed. His police (STF) had to arrest the former minister Sharma as the case was being monitored by the MP High Court. National papers like *Hindustan Times*, *The Indian Express*, and many TV channels talked about the scam extensively and indicated the possible involvement of the CM, as one of his personal assistants was also found involved in the scam and was arrested. Congress leaders like Satyadev Katare, leader of Opposition in the Assembly and KK Mishra, party spokesman alleged that phone calls were made from the CM's House to Vyapam officials to accommodate certain candidates. *Hindustan Times* Bhopal edition carried a story 'Queen of Controversy' with a photograph of Sadhana Singh, the CM's wife, pointing to the fact that she had a hand in the scam, though it was never proved.

Congress leaders who made an accusation that she was directly involved in the scam, got a quick defamation notice in the last week of June, the time when the CM found himself in a tight spot, for the first time during his eight-year rule. This was perhaps the worst political crisis of his career. His worries reflected in the surprise shifting of his principal secretary Manoj Shrivastava and return of Iqbal Singh Bains from deputation to the Government of India. Bains had ably served in the same position earlier and is a well-known confidante of Shivraj.

In and out of the state assembly, the CM had to bear the brunt of the attack almost alone. But thanks to his astute management, he won a reprieve from the central leadership, as well as from the RSS.

He went to Mohankhera, a Jain pilgrim centre in Dhar district where the top RSS leadership's annual congregation took place and met with Dr Mohan Bhagwat to explain his side of the story. He was not among those who were invited there as it was a pure RSS event.

Earlier, he also met Narendra Modi on 27 June and clarified his stand that there were very few irregularities and when they came to light 'he and his government quickly swung into action' by arresting doctors, government officials, students, brokers and so on.

Talking to me at his residence sometime in July 2014, Shivraj said less than one per cent irregularities took place in over 3.50 lakh recruitments that were done over the years. He said that it was he who, working on an anonymous complaint, asked the Indore Inspector General of Police to probe the matter, sometime in June-July 2013, on the eve of the Assembly elections. 'I was the person who, after consulting Chief Secretary Anthony D'sa and DGP Nandan Dube, formed a Special Task Force (STF) and expedited the matter. The task Force's working was lauded by the Chief Justice of MP High Court which turned down a demand by some petitioners, including Congress leaders, of a probe into the scam by the CBI.'

## Mission 29-0

Well, on the political front he did well. The corruption charge notwithstanding, Shivraj Singh almost repeated a similar performance that he displayed in November 2013 state assembly elections in the Lok Sabha polls. The BJP in Madhya Pradesh had quickly got down to work after the resounding victory in the assembly and announced its mission of winning all 29 Lok Sabha seats from MP, something which had not happened ever before in the political history of Madhya Pradesh. Yes, after Indira Gandhi's assassination in 1984, under Arjun Singh's leadership, the Congress did bag all the 40 Lok Sabha seats of the undivided state. That happened mainly due to the strong sympathy wave that had swept the country following the Prime Minister's brutal killing. MP was no exception.

This time round, the BJP in Madhya Pradesh was benefitted from the powerful pro-Modi wave. Having got a free hand in picking candidates, BJP fielded as many as 14 new faces and one 'imported' from Congress (Hoshangabad) and all 15 won with handsome margins, not to talk of other stalwarts like Indore's Sumitra Mahajan (4.68 lakh) and Vidisha's Sushma Sawraj. While Sumitra Mahajan went on to become BJP's first Speaker of the Lok Sabha, Sushma Sawraj became an important minister in the Modi cabinet, heading the Ministry of External Affairs (MEA). Party President Narendra Singh Tomar too won a tough Gwalior seat and became a minister in Modi cabinet.

If Shivraj Singh could not complete his Mission-29, it was due to two Congress leaders. The two seats that went the Congress were won by Jyotiraditya Scindia in Guna and party veteran Kamal Nath from Chhindwara. Both have been winning these seats and if they withstood the Modi onslaught, it was purely due to their individual standing, better image and ground level contacts. They managed to insulate themselves from the Modi effect and completely sullen image of their own party.

Yet the BJP's show was superb in the sense that the winning margins of almost all BJP candidates were huge, thanks to meticulous planning of state BJP officials and endless campaign touring by Shivraj Singh. He showed no signs of fatigue after hectic, round-the-clock campaigning in the assembly elections. He told me once that he wanted to visit all 29 seats at least once before the code of conduct came into force. And he did it. It was during these whirlwind tours that he had spared me time for conversations for this book.

It was heartening for him that his pet schemes of 'beti bachao' (save the girl child) found a mention in Arun Jaitley's maiden union budget in July as the Modi government too showed keenness in adopting it at the all-India level. Later, Prime Minister Narendra Modi, speaking at the function of the Indian Council of Agriculture Research (ICAR) on 30 July in Delhi, stressed the importance of making agriculture a profitable business and called upon people to save water to bring about a 'blue revolution' to help farmers and fisheries business. The Union Government released close to ₹ 962 crore agriculture farm insurance to benefit 14 lakh peasants across Madhya Pradesh. The state government also added to it by giving ₹ 995 crore. Shivraj has already been working for the past many years on making agriculture as profitable business.

Madhya Pradesh's good work was being taken note of at the national level too, which added to Shivraj's stature in some way.

Shivraj's ultimate honour came when he was picked up by Modi to be made an important member of the Central Parliamentary Board in August, putting to end the rumour mills that were working over time. Since the exposure of the Vyapam scam, it was being talked about in political, bureaucratic, business and media circles that Shivraj would be eased out but that did not happen. Instead, he got elevated and found new recognition in a party headed by Gujarat's new president Amit Shah, the youngest to lead the BJP so far.

ଭଭଭଭ

# PROLOGUE

Some ideas spring out of cups of tea. On a quiet Sunday morning during my posting in Aurangabad (Maharashtra), between sips of tea, I called up a veteran journalist friend in Bhopal. After brief pleasantries, I asked him, "Is there a scope for a book in English on the Madhya Pradesh Chief Minister Shivraj Singh Chouhan?"

My friend, an acclaimed political analyst and writer instantly countered: "Why don't you write one?"

By sheer coincidence, I had recently finished reading political biographies of Gujarat Chief Minister Narendra Modi and his Bihar counterpart Nitish Kumar, among others.

My umbilical links have been with Mumbai but I belong to Madhya Pradesh and am deeply attached to the land and its people. Throughout my Maharashtra assignment, the pull for Madhya Pradesh would keep dragging me back, mentally if not physically. I had a natural and emotional bond with Indore and the state where my career as a journalist had blossomed through three decades.

Madhya Pradesh is traditionally perceived as a 'backward' state even if it has never been as backward as Odisha and Bihar were at one time. With its largely amiable and violence-free disposition, it has come to be seen as a politically stable state. It wasn't much heard and talked about on the national level. After the '80s, it slowly came to be known for PC Sethi, former Railways and Home Minsiter, Arjun Singh and Digvijay Singh, and before that for DP Mishra, the Shukla brothers—Shyama Charan and Vidya Charan and Rajmata

Vijayaraje Scindia—players well-known on the national circuit. But unlike its neighbours Maharashtra, Uttar Pradesh or Gujarat, MP seldom hogged national headlines—for good reasons or otherwise.

Elections to the State Assembly in Madhya Pradesh were still a few months away when I returned to Bhopal from Maharashtra in the latter half of 2013. Speculation was rife over the prospects of Shivraj Singh-led Bharatiya Janata Party (BJP) retaining power with a facile win. The main Opposition party hardly posed a threat thanks to its execrable squabbles and feeble leadership. The Congress was already out of power for 10 years (2003-13) courtesy former Chief Minister Digvijay Singh's pathetic record of governance in the 'BIMARU' state.

These and some other political factors had ignited in my mind the idea of a book on Chouhan and Madhya Pradesh. But some strange inhibition coupled with my routine journalistic engagements in Maharashtra kept me from starting the project. My friends did not prod me either. The thought of the book thus got shelved temporarily.

However, about three months ahead of the 25 November Assembly polls, electioneering had already taken off. The BJP was going about its task quite methodically. Shivraj Singh was in striking form. Simultaneously though tension was building up within the BJP at the national level. The tremors of the Goa and Delhi events of September 2013 were being felt elsewhere. The 'party with a difference' appeared to be split between the former strong man LK Advani and the fast emerging challenger, Modi. Narendra Modi, or NaMo as he was nicknamed by the media, had already pitchforked himself as a national leader. With solid backing by the Rashtriya Swayamsewak Sangh (RSS), he persuaded the BJP to announce him the prime ministerial candidate. Shivraj Singh Chouhan, an otherwise reticent and low-profile leader, was somewhat averse to the idea of Modi being named for the top job before the five states went to polls. He had his own reasons, compulsions and calculations for it. One of them was the apprehension of the Muslim support base that he had built with his liberal image eroding in the state if Modi were to campaign. Shivraj had cultivated the minorities with his moderate image over the years.

Having won comfortably in 2008 (within three years of becoming the CM), Shivraj was hopeful of achieving an unprecedented hat-trick for the BJP through his own efforts. Clearly he was eager to make history in a big state like MP.

As the election date drew closer and with the Congress presenting the youthful face of Jyotiraditya Scindia, scion of the erstwhile Gwalior royal family and son of former Union minister late Madhavrao Scindia, it appeared the BJP would find it tough to form a government for the third time in a row. There were talks of anti-incumbency factor against several 'tainted' ministers and MLAs of the ruling party. Scales started tilting and it appeared that there would be a close contest between the traditional rivals. Some serving and former bureaucrats also felt the BJP would just scrape through to form the government. Even the serving bureaucrats in districts and other places did not back the ruling party to bag more than 110-120 seats. A former DGP called me up after the polling and forecast a 'hung Assembly'. A former chief secretary also felt the BJP was not faring too well. Local media, businessmen and independent observers were heard talking of 'a possible change'. To be honest I also felt the Congress was inching closer to the magic figure of 115, in an Assembly of 230, because of the overall 'feedback' from all over the state.

But that was not to be! Shivraj Singh Chouhan's rustic magic worked even beyond his own expectations, taking the tally to 165 when the results were announced on 8 December 2013. The Congress that had dreamt of forming the government was reduced to a meagre 58 seats, the second lowest in history, down by 13 seats from 2008. The BJP had scored a hat-trick, riding the charisma of Shivraj Singh who had touched the pinnacle of his popularity.

The comprehensive victory not only made Shivraj the Chief Minister for a record third time, but instantly catapulted him into the national reckoning, alongside the high profile and aggressive 'NaMo', whose claim to the prime ministerial candidacy was reinforced by BJP's 4-1 victory in state elections. He had addressed many election meetings across MP as also in other states. Superficially, at least the BJP's 'rift' was not visible to an outsider in the fast-changing scenario in Delhi. But Shivraj quickly came to terms with his new-found stardom on the saffron horizon and remained grounded.

## Hat-trick Heroes

In the annals of Indian politics, there are several other chief ministers who have scored hat-tricks. In fact, there are at least 10-11 such political heroes in different states from different political outfits. Pawan Kumar Chamling of Sikkim Democratic Front and Tarun Gogoi of the Congress have continued as Chief Ministers since 1994 and 2001; Meghalaya's CM, Capt Williamson Sangma, has been around for six times between 1970 and 1983—first as leader of the All Party Hill Leaders Conference (APHLC) and then as a Congressman; Tripura's Leftist leader Manik Sarkar, the 'original *aam aadmi*' of contemporary politics, due to his austere habits and low profile has been at the helm since 1998, to name a few.

If recent Assembly elections saw Sheila Dikshit lose her strong bastion after completing three full terms from 1998 to 2013 in Delhi, her lesser-known party colleague Lal Thanhawla sprang a surprise by successfully holding his fort in Mizoram. His victory was the sole consolation for the Congress in 2013.

But then this is not a story confined to the chief ministers of north-eastern region's lesser known and smaller states compared to the Hindi heartland satraps or of West Bengal, where the redoubtable Communist icon Jyoti Basu continued his reign from 1977 till 2000, a record yet to be broken by any party or individual in any state—23 long years. His successor, Buddhadeb Bhattacharjee also completed a long innings of 11 years (2000-2011) before bowing out to the fiery *'didi'* Mamata Banerjee who quit INC to form the Trinamool Congress, a regional outfit that upheld Bengali pride. In Chhattisgarh, a tiny state carved out of Madhya Pradesh in November 2000, with two other smaller states—Jharkhand from Bihar and Uttarakhand from UP—Dr Raman Singh (BJP) also managed to record a straight third win. He had first wrested power from a corrupt Ajit Jogi regime in 2003. He lost a number of seats, as also percentage of votes, yet retained power by a reduced margin of 10 seats (49-39). And, of course, there is Narendra Modi who, despite unprecedented media criticism and plethora of legal cases against him, comfortably won three terms, the first being in December 2002 and the third win coming in the autumn of 2012 which continues till date as his fourth term in office.

So, in such a political scenario, why is Shivraj Singh so special? And, why is MP different?

Well, it is for more than one reason! The sheer size of the 'BIMARU' state which even after bifurcation is pretty large—its own state highways are close to 11,000 km; about 3,08,000 sq km geographical area coupled with complex caste dynamics. The seven crore plus population poses peculiar problems; the land-locked state has boundaries touching Maharashtra (south), Gujarat (west), Rajasthan (north-west), UP (north) and Chhattisgarh (north-east). This by itself would give an idea of its size and the resultant issues. Some of its districts are located as far as 780 km (Singrauli) from capital Bhopal; or Anuppur (656 km) or Rewa (536 km). The sprawling state, with 29 Lok Sabha seats, has had a strong history of Congress domination since its birth on 1 November 1956 and before that too. The Congress hegemony was broken twice for brief interludes in 1977, 1990 and then for ten long years since 2003. The saffronisation of the state actually began in 2003 when *Sadhvi* Uma Bharti dislodged the 10-year-old Digvijay Singh regime with a record margin, winning as many as 173 seats and consigning the Congress to the dustbin of history. The opposition mustered a paltry 38 seats—its lowest ever!

If Shivraj Singh steered his party to a historic third straight win in December 2013, it is due to his personal charisma, clean image and a very fine blend of social engineering which he preached and practised for eight years, unlike his many contemporaries and predecessors!

In these times of demographic dividends, the nation has indeed taken notice of a much younger politician than the Prime Minister, Dr Manmohan Singh, or the BJP stalwart, Lal Krishna Advani.

This is the story of the rising regional sun...!

ଓଡ଼ଓଡ଼

# INTRODUCTION

If you are living in a remote corner of the country, say somewhere in Sriganganagar of Rajasthan, a village bordering Pakistan or somewhere in Tamil Nadu, you may hardly feel the need to know much about Madhya Pradesh, considered the heart of the nation. Such lack of newsworthiness is no longer a virtue in these times of hype and hoopla. Madhya Pradesh has, however, preferred a staid presence on the national scene.

Without any ostensible reason, the state was divided 14 years ago. Before bifurcation and creation of Chhattisgarh in 2000, however, Madhya Pradesh or MP as it is commonly known, was India's largest state in geographical expanse. A huge population of nearly seven crore gave its administrators enough socio-economic issues to worry about.

The present state, with its capital in Bhopal, came into being in 1956, under the states' reorganisation plan of the Government of India, nine years after Independence. But before 1956, its capital was Nagpur and it was still called Madhya Pradesh (Central Province), with southern parts of present-day MP and north-eastern districts of today's Maharashtra merging into it. Its last Chief Minister was Pt Ravi Shankar Shukla, who went on to become the first CM of MP in November 1956—a rare event in political history with someone heading two states as a Chief Minister during his lifetime.

Over their long rule, the British had captured a large number of the 562 small and big princely states of India, such as Mysore, Baroda, Gwalior, Indore, Kolhapur and Bhopal. Those falling in the central region were ceded in the Central Province and Berar (CP & Berar) and the Central India Agency. Berar represented the present-day Vidarbha of Maharashtra, where the separate statehood demand has simmered for a long time. Recently it was reignited after the Union Government decided to split neighbouring Andhra Pradesh and create Telangana. Incidentally Andhra Pradesh was created under Jawaharlal Nehru in October 1953, by hiving it off from Madras Presidency. Tamil Nadu also came into existence as a new state. It was after the protests that he announced in Parliament the formation of the States Reorganisation Commission (SRC) on 22 December 1953 under Justice Syed Fazal Ali. Its report came in October 1955.

However, in 1956, as per the recommendations of the States Reorganisation Commission (1955), the state was reorganised on linguistic basis and the geographical boundaries were drawn up afresh. The tiny Bhopal state, some parts of Mahakaushal, about 14 districts of Chhattisgarh, Vindhya Pradesh (inaugurated in 1948) and Madhya Bharat, were merged into one large Hindi-speaking state named Madhya Pradesh. It still exists but with the changes mentioned above—the south-eastern region parting to become Chhattisgarh in November 2000. Chhattisgarh was described by Sir Alexander Cunningham, the great archaeologist as 'Maha-Kosala, or great Kosala. It comprised the upper valley of the Mahanadi and its tributaries from source of the Narbudda (Narmada) at Amarkantaka on the north, to the source of the Mahanadi itself near Kanker on the south, from the valley of the Wainganga, on the west to the Hasdeo and Jonk rivers on the east.' According to Prabhu Lal Mishra (*The Political History of Chhattisgarh*), the frontiers described by Cunningham are the most acceptable ones and other scholars like RB Hiralal and CV Vaidya have accepted these.

This little historical perspective, I feel, is required to understand the present-day MP, which is yet to be emotionally merged into one-state-one-soul entity like any other southern state, say Kerala or Tamil Nadu, or northern states such as Punjab and Haryana where the regional pride and cohesion are well-defined.

Legally and geographically different parts of erstwhile CP and Berar were woven into one state almost six decades ago, yet in today's Madhya Pradesh, there continues to exist a Malwa region (Indore, Ujjain, etc); a Mahakoshal (Jabalpur, Mandla, Chhindwara); a Vindhya Pradesh (Rewa, Satna, Singrauli, etc); a Bundelkhand (Sagar, Panna, Tikamgarh, etc) and the Gwalior-Chambal (Morena, Bhind, Shivpuri). Moreover, local people often fondly refer to these regions by their names rather than 'Madhya Pradesh' in informal talks.

Arjun Singh, for example, was always seen—within the state—as a leader from the Vindhya, as is his son Ajay Singh, a senior MLA and a former minister. Late Madhavrao Scindia was treated as the leader of the Gwalior-Chambal area, though he was a national figure just like Arjun Singh who had become Governor of Punjab in 1985 but later quit the decorative post to enter the Lok Sabha from New Delhi. Union minister of many years' standing, Kamal Nath is still considered a leader of just Chhindwara, a Lok Sabha constituency. In the pre-bifurcation days, both the Shukla brothers, Shyama Charan and Vidya Charan (sons of Ravi Shankar Shukla), were 'leaders of Chhattisgarh' despite Madhya Pradesh having already become an important political entity. Late VC Shukla was at the forefront of the people demanding statehood for Chhattisgarh, though his elder brother and former CM of MP, Shyama Charan, had personally told me a few times about his opposition to breaking up the state.

With such a social-political background, MP has its own unique beauty, illustrious history and unbeatable charm. This may not be 'God's own country' but it certainly is second to none.

Well-known poet-writer, late Dom Moraes, after extensively travelling the length and breadth of the undivided Madhya Pradesh had observed the following in his famous book of the '80s—*Answered by Flutes*: 'Questions filled my mind…I thought of everything I had done in my life…and what my further destinations would be… perhaps, only in Madhya Pradesh could I have received some form of reply…all the birds cried out together and from the trees and forested slopes of the mountains I was answered and told to be happy by myriad unquestioning flutes'.

The diversity of MP is truly remarkable. It has the 1,000-year old amazing erotic sculptural splendour in the temples of Khajuraho and the world-famous Buddhist pilgrimage at Sanchi; it has verdant jungles that provide a wonderful habitat to a flying squirrel as well as to a Royal Bengal tiger. It can boast of the sacred river Narmada and of course, the gorgeous mountain ranges of Satpura and Vindhyachal! Mother Nature has truly been very kind to this region.

The state's peaceful record has fortunately remained intact by and large barring a few sporadic incidents. Its political traditions have provided the necessary stability for growth, unlike in states like Uttar Pradesh where four or five political parties scramble for power and relegate development issues to the background or the Maharashtra of the '90s. Madhya Pradesh was not an exception when the post-Mandal Commission churning led to the birth of an entirely new brand of political leadership in many states. Many gamechangers have emerged on the nation's political canvas since 1990 and hastened a social transformation.

Political parties that were dominated by upper castes gradually underwent a change in leadership pattern. Many modern leaders realised the vision that was conjured up by the Mandal Commission.

Lalu Yadav, Nitish Kumar, Mulayam Singh, Mayawati, Uma Bharti, Narendra Modi, or Shivraj—they represent the wide spectrum of a new India. Modi, Nitish Kumar and Shivraj Singh Chouhan deserve special mention for having brought about the paradigm shift in their political approach to developing a state.

In Madhya Pradesh, Digvijay Singh, a Thakur, could perhaps go down as the last sentinel of upper caste politics. His replacement marked the end of an era where Brahmins or Thakurs called the shots. Of the 18 chief ministers MP has seen, most were either Brahmins or Thakurs, for instance Govind Narayan Singh, DP Mishra, SC Shukla (three times), Arjun Singh, Digvijay Singh or Sunderlal Patwa (a Jain) and Kailash Joshi.

I am not a political crystal-gazer. But I feel the widespread changes affected by the current socio-economic churning in the political cauldron of the country are too significant to be overlooked by anyone—least of all, by policy makers and analysts. They are bound to leave a lasting mark on the socio-political and economic scenario.

Shivraj Singh Chouhan, a Kirar, a small OBC community in MP, has imparted a modern, vibrant image to the state. If his well-documented claims are correct, Madhya Pradesh has risen out of the BIMARU class in about eight years of his rule. In fact, it is now a new home to the Green Revolution, relegating Punjab, Haryana and Maharashtra to much lower rungs in agricultural diversity and growth. Both Prof Ashish Bose (who coined the BIMARU acronym) and Dr MS Swaminathan (the father of Green Revolution) would like to see for themselves, the striking metamorphosis in this central Indian state—the heart of India.

ଉଉଉଉ

## AT THE HELM FROM 1956

| No. | Name | Period |
|---|---|---|
| 1. | Shri Ravishankar Shukla | 01.11.1956 to 31.12.1956 |
| 2. | Shri Bhagwantrao Mandloi | 01.01.1957 to 30.01.1957 |
| 3. | Dr. Kailashnath Katju | 31.01.1957 to 14.04.1957 |
| 4. | Dr. Kailashnath Katju | 15.04.1957 to 11.03.1962 |
| 5. | Shri Bhagwantrao Mandloi | 12.03.1962 to 29.09.1963 |
| 6. | Shri Dwarka Prasad Mishra | 30.09.1963 to 08.03.1967 |
| 7. | Shri Dwarka Prasad Mishra | 09.03.1967 to 29.07.1967 |
| 8. | Shri Govindnarayan Singh | 30.07.1967 to 12.03.1969 |
| 9. | Shri Raja Nareshchandra Singh | 13.03.1969 to 25.03.1969 |
| 10. | Shri Shyamacharan Shukla | 26.03.1969 to 28.01.1972 |
| 11. | Shri Prakash Chandra Sethi | 29.01.1972 to 22.03.1972 |
| 12. | Shri Prakash Chandra Sethi | 23.03.1972 to 22.12.1975 |
| 13. | Shri Shyamacharan Shukla | 23.12.1975 to 29.04.1977 |
| * | **President's Rule** | **30.04.1977 to 25.06.1977** |
| 14. | Shri Kailash Chandra Joshi | 26.06.1977 to 17.01.1978 |
| 15. | Shri Virendra Kumar Sakhlecha | 18.01.1978 to 19.01.1980 |
| 16. | Shri Sunderlal Patwa | 20.01.1980 to 17.02.1980 |
| * | **President's Rule** | **18.02.1980 to 08.06.1980** |
| 17. | Shri Arjun Singh | 09.06.1980 to 10.03.1985 |
| 18. | Shri Arjun Singh | 11.03.1985 to 12.03.1985 |
| 19. | Shri Motilal Vora | 13.03.1985 to 13.02.1988 |
| 20. | Shri Arjun Singh | 14.02.1988 to 24.01.1989 |
| 21. | Shri Motilal Vora | 25.01.1989 to 08.12.1989 |
| 22. | Shri Shyamacharan Shukla | 09.12.1989 to 04.03.1990 |
| 23. | Shri Sunderlal Patwa | 05.03.1990 to 15.12.1992 |
| * | **President's Rule** | **16.12.1992 to 06.12.1993** |
| 24. | Shri Digvijay Singh | 07.12.1993 to 01.12.1998 |
| 25. | Shri Digvijay Singh | 01.12.1998 to 08.12.2003 |
| 26. | Sushri Uma Bharti | 09.12.2003 to 23.08.2004 |
| 27. | Shri Babulal Gaur | 24.08.2004 to 29.11.2005 |
| 28. | Shri Shivraj Singh Chouhan | 30.11.2005 to 12.12.2008 |
| 29. | Shri Shivraj Singh Chouhan | 13.12.2008 to 13.12.2014 |
| 30. | Shri Shivraj Singh Chouhan | 14.12.2013 **and continuing** |

Chapter - 1

# THE MAKING OF SHIVRAJ JAIT TO JAIL

It was a wintry morning for Prem Singh Chouhan, a marginal farmer of a tiny village Jait in the Sehore district of Madhya Pradesh. He was waiting for his farm labourers, although he had not been able to grow much due to a near-total absence of power and irrigation facilities in those days; even the shepherds had not turned up to take out the cattle for grazing.

Prem Singh was in his mid-thirties. His full-time work was to oversee cultivation of land he had inherited from his father, to make two ends meet for a large joint family consisting of four brothers and their children. That was the only source of income for the Chouhan family. They were not big landlords, yet were not poor farmers either.

When he made inquiries why the labourers of his farm as well as those of the adjoining ones had not turned up that morning, Prem Singh discovered that a young boy of his own family had stopped them from going to work. The boy was trying to unite them against what he thought was 'grave injustice'; the boy wanted the labourers' daily wages doubled. Curiously, a demand like this in that small village was raised when words like 'agitation', 'strike', 'labour charge hike', etc were alien to the innocent and mostly illiterate villagers. But the young boy went ahead with a protest rally with a handful

2  *Shivraj Singh And Rise Of Madhya Pradesh*

of bonded labourers joining it. Some of them were much older than him in age and did not even know what they were doing. At the local temple the next day, a meeting was also convened to chalk out 'future strategy' but no one showed up. The meeting turned out to be a 'big flop'.

Prem Singh, now 79, wittily recalls, "*Hamare he khilaph chupchap mazdooron ki hadtal karva dali thi usne; kaise kar sakta tha woh ye sab.*" (He had secretly organised a strike of the labourers against us; how could he?) The young boy was scolded, put under 'house arrest' and later shifted to Bhopal to be with his uncle Chain Singh who was a lower division clerk in the MP Board of Secondary Education, commonly known as the 'Board'.

No prizes for guessing who the young 'leader' was! Shivraj Singh Chouhan, who registered a hat-trick in December 2013 by becoming the central Indian state's Chief Minister for the third time in a row. He has now metamorphosed into one of the stalwarts of the rightist formation, Bharatiya Janata Party (BJP), at the national level, the one whose pro-poor policies and the art of governance are being discussed and emulated in non-BJP-ruled states as well.

Was the young, uneducated Shivraj, a leader-in-the-making? At a very young age, he had indeed demonstrated exemplary leadership qualities. The poverty of his fellow villagers and the 'injustice' and 'unfair' treatment of the farm workers had a deep-seated impact on this school-going boy. He could not stand hardships of the poor people who used to toil the whole day for paltry sums. They would begin work in the wee hours of winter mornings with scanty clothes to beat the cold. In those days, the barter system of exchanging goods and services was still prevalent in India's backward villages. Jait was no exception. And Shivraj was just about 10 years old then.

His father was not a great sympathizer of the then Jan Sangh or of the RSS. Like any father, however, he was trying to provide his son a modest education within his means which would later have fetched him a decent job.

The village, about 70 km from the capital, Bhopal, had a population of less than 600. Prem Singh said, the first primary school in Jait had been opened in 1952, after Sehore district got freedom from the erstwhile Bhopal state's Muslim rulers, a couple of years after India's Independence. Located right on the banks of the mighty Narmada river, Jait was a nondescript village which shot into fame only after Shivraj Singh Chouhan became the Chief Minister for the first time in November 2005.

Prem Singh now lives with another son in Bhopal in his own modest house in Saket Nagar on the outskirts of the city but does not throw his weight around as a CM's father. There is no security at his private house and no signs of an important person staying there. Interestingly, he recalls how even a peon of the erstwhile Bhopal *riyasat* (princely state of Nawab Hamidullah Khan, the last ruler) would be treated like a very important person (VIP) in their village. *Hum log to chhote log the aur Mughal riyasat ka koi banda gaon me aata tha to gaonwalon ko to dar hi lagta tha* (We were simple people with no clout; therefore, we would be scared whenever even a peon from the Muslim state visited the village). Such was the terror of the state. People from Jait and adjoining villages would avoid visiting Bhopal and preferred to go to Hoshangabad if necessary.

The Nawab-ruled Bhopal was a relatively well-administered state. Its uniqueness lay in the fact that it had been ruled even by four *Begums* (women rulers), the last being Sultana Jahan (1901-1926). She was the mother of Hamidullah Khan, the 13th and last ruler of Bhopal, which was, after Hyderabad and Junagarh, the third most important Muslim state in the India of the mid-20th century. It

## 4  *Shivraj Singh And Rise Of Madhya Pradesh*

had been founded in 1715 and was merged with the Indian Union in 1949 but Hamidullah Khan (1926-1960) remained the titular Nawab until his death in 1960.

## Shivraj Becomes Monitor

When Shivraj arrived in Bhopal on 'punishment' by his father, he did not like the city. "I was happy in my village and the *shahar ka vatavaran pehle mujhe pasand nahi aaya aur laga ki wapas gaon chale….* (I did not initially like the city's atmosphere and thought of returning to the village)." But he stayed on and joined the Gujarati School for a year in the 5th standard; he then moved to a Government School in Shivaji Nagar (6th to 8th standard). His first step on the ladder of leadership, as it turned out, was the Government Model School. At first, the young Shivraj did not like it much, but it changed his destiny forever. He became the monitor in the 7th standard and gave his first speech. Since Jait was situated on the bank of Narmada river, many holy men and monks visited the place regularly. There was a religious atmosphere in the village. *Akhand Ramayan Path, Narmada Puran,* Lord Ganesh and Goddess Durga's *poojas* were important functions which took place round the year. Since his childhood, he was fond of reading and quite early in his youth he had read the *Bhagavad Gita* and had memorised it thoroughly, perhaps due to the influence of his religious surroundings. So from a very young age, his bent of mind was religious but not tilted towards Hindu fundamentalism.

Shivraj was now flowering. The way he had shown his dislike for oppression of the weaker sections and some rebellious qualities at a very young age, it was obvious that he had innate leadership traits which blossomed in Bhopal over the next few years.

*The Making of Shivraj: Jait to Jail*    5

Dr Padmakar Tripathi, a physician in Bhopal, recalls his friendship with Shivraj during their Model School days where they were together in the last few years of schooling. Dr Tripathi says that Shivraj was a very active student and wanted to do something for the school and his co-students. So he contested the election for the *Sahitya Sachiv's* (Literary Secretary) post but lost it. During his college days, and later, he would always think of the welfare of the people and the society. "I had seen the restlessness within him those days. He was willing to work in slum areas to help people come out of their miseries," said Dr Tripathi.

Another schoolmate, Nitin Nandgaonkar, now an administrative officer in the finance department at the State Government's Secretariat, recalled that Shivraj did not get demoralised and fought the Student Union President's election the very next year (1974-75). This time he won by a massive margin. In a conversation with the author, Shivraj recalled the exact number of votes he had polled—1,198 of the 1,300. Nangdaonkar, who was on the panel as the Cultural Secretary says that Shivraj did not spend a single rupee on the election and his slogans were all pro-students. "He was a fluent speaker and would hold us spellbound with his language, choice of words, knowledge and overall eloquence," he recalled.

He was good in studies, oratory, was well-read and also bold. "Once we were on our way to Goa on a school trip," Nandgaonkar narrated, "when suddenly one of the wheels of our speeding bus got unhinged while it was passing through a *ghat* with frequent bends and turns. Shivraj showed exemplary presence of mind and courage; he jumped out of the running bus and rolled a big boulder in front of the bus to make it halt. The bus driver, Sharief, was flabbergasted but Shivraj's daring act saved the students and teachers from a close

## 6 *Shivraj Singh And Rise Of Madhya Pradesh*

shave with death. The mishap could have been very serious. One of his teachers, MK Shrivastava, also narrated this incident to me. Shrivastava was the English and Science teacher at Model School and fondly remembers his meritorious student who had helped him once after he became the CM. "Shivraj helped me after my retirement from the school in 2008 and treated me with respect at his house where I had gone for the first and last time." He noted that there was no change in the humility he had seen in the young Shivraj, as his student.

## A Political Worker

While he was still in the school's final year, the Jayaprakash Narayan-led students' movement had already begun in Bihar and spread like wildfire all over the country. The students' agitation that JP launched was also targeting the lacunae in the existing education system, besides issues like corruption and inflation. Shivraj, the natural leader, even in the midst of his studies, got irresistibly drawn into JP's agitation.

This was the time when the Jan Sangh, the earlier *avatar* of today's BJP, was talking of a ban on cow slaughter and other rightist issues. The Jan Sangh ideology touched an emotional chord in a flowering Shivraj. His last days in the school coincided with the imposition of the Emergency (June 1975-March 1977), the first of its kind since the Independence, by the then Prime Minister, Indira Gandhi. All the democratic institutions were rendered ineffective and the whole country seemed to be under the jackboot of the Congress Party.

A number of socio-political events were happening across the country. Bhopal was no exception. Even the sleepy town offered Shivraj an opportunity to become a political activist. Babulal Gaur, a

*The Making of Shivraj: Jait to Jail*    7

labour leader, was contesting a by-election from Bhopal's Govindpura seat on a *Teer-Kaman* (Bow-and-Arrow) symbol as an Independent candidate. He defeated Bhai Ratan Kumar of the Congress by over 12,000 votes. Shivraj, as a young volunteer, had enthusiastically and spontaneously worked for Gaur's victory. As fate would have it, Shivraj succeeded Gaur as the Chief Minister in 2005! Gaur lasted barely a year as the CM but Shivraj continues!

The Govindpura poll was Shivraj's first experience to be part of a serious political campaign. JP had given a clarion call to defeat the Congress and Shivraj realised that his political leaning was getting defined.

As things turned out in quick succession, a senior Jan Sangh functionary, Babulal Bhanpur, made him a member of the party with which he had found an instant emotional bond. He was impressed with their opposition to cow slaughter, perhaps because of his rural-agricultural background. Much later, Shivraj told me: "It was Jan Sangh and its ideology which I thought—although subliminally —was suited to my way of thinking... I detested the Congress."

Upon joining the Jan Sangh, he came close to the RSS through Vibhishanji who, impressed as he was with the hard-working young man, introduced him to several RSS leaders. It was then that he became a formal member of the Akhil Bharatiya Vidyarthi Parishad (ABVP), the student wing of the RSS. The Jan Sangh office was located near Peer Gate in Old Bhopal. Arif Baig, Dr Satya Narayan Jatiya, now an RSS member, and (late) Laxmi Narayan Sharma were the seniors Shivraj got a chance to work with in this office. He may not have sold tea at a stall but did all the menial jobs in the office and learnt from his seniors the art of organisation.

But life was not all smooth. A number of RSS, Jan Sangh and socialist leaders had been packed into jails during the Emergency

## 8 Shivraj Singh And Rise Of Madhya Pradesh

under the draconian new law—Maintenance of Internal Security Act (MISA). There was an all-pervasive atmosphere of fear and indignation. Those opposing the suspension of democratic rights and excesses of the Congress under Indira Gandhi were being targeted. While many had been rounded up on the then Chief Minister, PC Sethi's orders, a good number of Jan Sangh workers were still outside jail working underground. Ironically, the then Chief Secretary, Sushil Chandra Verma, IAS, who would report the daily updates on the arrests of Opposition leaders to the CM, later joined the BJP and became Bhopal's Member of Parliament for four successive terms between 1989 and 1998. Verma defeated the former Indian cricket captain, Mansoor Ali Khan Pataudi (having family links with Bhopal) and Arif Baig, among others. Baig, who was in the Jan Sangh while Shivraj was a political toddler in the party, had switched to the Congress in the 1990s, only to return to the BJP fold. It was Shivraj Singh as CM in 2013 who granted the septuagenarian Muslim leader, a BJP ticket from Bhopal (North) constituency. While Baig lost, the BJP, riding piggyback on the massive Shivraj wave, returned to power a third time.

An energetic and young Shivraj was among those working underground during the Emergency. "I used to distribute cyclostyled pamphlets against the Emergency and Indira Gandhi, and paste them in public toilets and other places. We would get the pamphlets delivered at a tea stall run by Nathuram Soni who was also a Jan Sangh sympathiser," he recalls.

Shivraj had no idea that he was skating on thin ice. The 'underground' work could not have gone unnoticed for a long time. One evening, while he was studying for his 11th class examination scheduled to commence two days later, the police knocked on his door around eight in the evening. He was not prepared for this as

The Making of Shivraj: Jait to Jail    9

he was not doing anything overtly to attract police attention. He was still only a 16-year-old school boy. When the Habibganj police station sub-inspector Pingle saw the young Shivraj, he was surprised and told his colleagues that the lad was unlikely to be working against Indira Gandhi and that they had perhaps got a wrong name and address. He asked Shivraj a few questions and appeared convinced that they had knocked on the wrong door. As they were about to leave, a constable in the police party suggested they search his room. The discovery of pamphlets and other 'objectionable' material was sufficient evidence and the police promptly dragged him out of his small room and lodged him in the Bhopal jail.

The police had just a few days ago arrested Suryakant Kelkar, the ABVP chief then and in his diary Shivraj's name was scribbled somewhere as the parishad's volunteer. This was how the police got a whiff about Shivraj.

One day he was thrashed, abused and asked to tender an apology to help him get released from jail. He refused. Even while being taken in an auto-rickshaw to the police station and then to jail, Shivraj was shouting slogans against the government, something that 'worsened' his case further. In jail, he was among the youngest. Other leaders included the socialist Sharif Master, Jan Sangh's Laxmi Narayan Sharma, Babulal Gaur, Arif Baig, and some leaders from the Jamaat-e-Islami, Arya Samaj and Anand Marg as well.

The MISA detention helped him in two ways: one, his internal resolve to do something for the society and the nation got strengthened and, tow, he got the great company of scholarly people in the jail from whom he could learn a lot and develop his personality. "Gauri Shankar Kaushalji would read out and perform *sandhya*, a daily evening religious ritual, and then we would read the *Bhagavad Gita* in groups and discuss it. I had some copies left after my grandfather's death which my relatives had brought to jail. I got deeply involved in it and understood the holy book much better in the prison. I also read Lokmanya Tikak's epic *Gita Rahasya*, which the great freedom fighter wrote while in Mandale Jail, and *Sant Gyaneshwar*. All this had a lasting impact on my personality." The foundation of Shivraj's great oratory were laid in that jail.

The *Gita* taught him a lot: "You have a right to action, not to its fruits; let the fruits not be the motive of your work...giving up the fruits of work means not to perform work for the good of one's own mind and body."

However, while he was 'enjoying' the prison's atmosphere and benefitted immensely from scholarly discussions that sharpened his mind and opened new vistas, a tragedy happened. "Under the Defence of India Rules (DIR), I, being a minor, was being repeatedly taken to court." During one of the visits, his grandmother who was very fond of him spotted him with the police. "She cried thinking I had done something terribly wrong." When she first heard it in Jait, she could not believe that her innocent, honest grandson could go to jail. She repeatedly asked her son Prem Singh about it. What offence did her little sweetheart commit? Gomatibai could not resist and one day reached the jail in Bhopal with her son. Since he was being taken to court, she could see him and cried inconsolably. Young Shivraj was deeply moved. In 1976, she passed away.

Her death shattered Shivraj. "My hatred for Indira Gandhi seemed heightened due to the personal tragedy."

ଉ୍ଥଉ୍ଥ

Chapter - 2

# SHIVRAJ, THE POLITICIAN

Shaligram Shrivastava, an Independent MLA from Budni, Meghraj Jain of the Bhartiya Janata Yuva Morcha, besides Kushabhau Thakre, the doyen of the Jan Sangh and later the BJP, were among the early influences on young Shivraj as a political worker in his formative years. Later, Pyarelal Khandelwal, Narayan Gupta and Sunderlal Patwa were the leaders who groomed him.

But Thakre has a special place in Shivraj's life for more reasons than one. Kushabhau, who hailed from Dhar near Indore and lived in Gwalior for most part of his initial years, was among the first batch of RSS full-time *pracharakas* to have been sent to the Jan Sangh. The Rashtriya Swayamsewak Sangh's longest-serving *Sarasanghchalak* (chief), Guruji Golwalkar (Madhav Sadashiv Golwalkar—RSS head from June 1940-June 1973) had handpicked Thakre to work for the Jan Sangh, the political wing of the RSS. During the Emergency, he was lodged in Begumganj prison under MISA while Shivraj was in Bhopal jail but Shivraj was already feeling drawn to him, such was Thakre's personality.

By the time the Emergency was lifted in 1977 and elections announced, Thakre had become an important leader in the Jan Sangh. Shivraj, having seen him from a distance, was very impressed

## 12 Shivraj Singh And Rise Of Madhya Pradesh

with Thakre. Kushabhau was elected the president of the Jan Sangh unanimously in August 1977 and remained so till its merger with the BJP in December 1980. Kushabhau, a life-long bachelor, was an extremely simple and a pure soul, rare to find in today's politics. His frugal lifestyle had become a hallmark of any politician's lifestyle. As a father figure of the BJP, he is credited with grooming a large number of leaders in MP such as Sunderlal Patwa, Kailash Sarang, Kailash Joshi, Lakhhiram Agarwal, Sumitra Mahajan (she was also influenced by Rajmata Vijayaraje Scindia) and Vikram Verma, to name just a few. Thakre is also remembered for taking the Jan Sangh-BJP roots very deep in Madhya Pradesh at a time when the Congress had complete sway over the state.

Thakre, however, was not the one who could take to electoral politics like a fish to water. When the party asked him, he reluctantly contested a Lok Sabha by-election from Khandwa in 1979 and defeated Shivkumar Singh during the Janata Party's government at the Centre but he was quintessentially an organisation man all through his political life. He was fielded by the party again in the 1980 General Elections, only to lose to the same candidate of the Congress—Shivkumar Singh who he had trounced a year ago. That was his last date with electoral politics.

Much later he went on to become the national president of the BJP from 1998-2000 when Atal Bihari Vajpayee-led NDA was in power in Delhi. He wielded considerable influence in those days and succeeded LK Advani who had joined the Union Government. It was Thakre who had in 1998 made Narendra Modi the party's national general secretary. Kushabhau's simplicity was exemplary: he would never have a beacon light atop his old Ambassador car nor would he have any police security van piloting him on his tours, despite his party being in power in Delhi. Compared to his national

*Shivraj, The Politician* 13

counterpart Sonia Gandhi, he was completely down to earth in every sense of the term. The day he was going by car to Indore, with his party in power in Delhi, Sonia as the head of the Opposition had arrived in a helicopter at Mandsaur, accompanied by at least four separate choppers ferrying top Congress leaders for an election rally in 1998, which I had covered then. The stark contrast between the two national party presidents is still fresh in my mind. Shorn of all the trappings that power brings with it, Thakre had actually set an example in political life. Alas, many of his party men do not seem to emulate him today! He would never flaunt his position. I had seen him stopping his car at a toll booth in Dewas to pay tax on the way from Bhopal to Indore, soon after addressing a press conference at the party's state headquarters. He would not heed requests from TV anchors and reporters to change his 'dull kurta' to appear 'smart' on the TV screens.

No surprise then that Shivraj was attracted towards Thakre many years ago. *"Mujhe unse milne ke bad, unki karyashaili aur imandari dekhne ke bad aise laga jaise woh he mere jeevan ka adarsh ho sakenge,"* he told me once (after meeting him and watching his honest way of working, thinking style, I thought he was the ideal for me in my public life). However, unlike Thakre or others in the Jan Sangh and the BJP, Shivraj rarely attended the RSS daily *shakhas*. He did complete the Officers Training Camp (OTC) in 1980-81, but rarely attended the morning or evening *shakhas* with Vibhishan Singh in Bhopal.

When the Janata Party was formed and the Emergency was gone, Shaligram Shrivastava took him under his wing to set up the base of the party in the remote areas of Vidisha, Raisen and Sehore districts of the Bhopal division and to erect some kind of primary organisational structure in those areas to woo the people to the

14    *Shivraj Singh And Rise Of Madhya Pradesh*

Janata Party as workers. Budni, from where he made his debutant entry into the State Assembly in 1990, did not have any trace of the Jan Sangh or the BJP for years before his victory. In 1980 when Raghavji Bhai unsuccessfully contested Lok Sabha poll from Vidisha, he lost heavily from the Budni segment. In 1984 he repeated the same 'performance', from Vidisha but this time around, the reason for the defeat was different. In October 1984, Prime Minister Indira Gandhi had been assassinated and the elections thereafter saw the Congress riding the sympathy wave and winning all the 40 LS seats of undivided Madhya Pradesh under Chief Minister Arjun Singh's leadership. It was a record of sorts in the political history of MP.

Arjun Singh (considered the shrewdest CM the state had seen) had a vision for development and had many firsts to his credit, but he could complete only one full term in office and then became an all-India leader in Delhi.

Shivraj had not completed his college education when Raghavji Bhai was contesting his first election. While working as a full-time ABVP volunteer (later its regional organisation secretary), he took admission in Saifia College first and then shifted to Hamidia College in Bhopal for his graduation (Bachelor of Arts) degree that he passed in first class, despite being occupied full time with politics and student activities. He used to work for the party organisation throughout the day and burn the midnight oil literally. Having passed his 11th standard with distinction in science and physics, an intelligent student like him would have perhaps gone for the medical or engineering stream but he chose lighter subjects, perhaps because of his attraction towards public life, a decision he never regretted.

Since Budni *tehsil* was close to his Jait village, he chose to work there first with Shaligram Shrivastava in his 1977 election and then in the Lok Sabha polls of Raghavji Bhai in 1980. Thanks to his work

*Shivraj, The Politician* 15

in the field (where he had also organised a strike of the forest workers against the department's officials), he instantly earned popularity badly required for any political leader. "When he invited me I was surprised as he was trying to show me Budni where we had no base; I went reluctantly only to see a crowd of over 3,000-4,000 people from areas around listening to him in rapt attention… he was standing on the poles of the forest office gate and was addressing the people and shouting against the Congress government," Meghraj Jain told me in conversation at his home one day.

Shivraj's hard work translated into success. In 1984 though Raghavji Bhai lost the election, Budni provided him some lead. Shivraj had also invited former CM, Sunderlal Patwa, the first BJP president in MP (Dec 1980-Nov 1983) to Budni for the forest workers and peasants' rally but Patwa admonished him and stayed away without any conceivable reason. Perhaps he had doubts about Shivraj's capability to garner a crowd in the small place. Patwa was known to be a tough guy and his language could turn acerbic at times.

The little success that Shivraj got on his own was enough to motivate him tremendously. His work was also getting recognised at the state level where the party bigwigs were passing through a tough phase having lost the General and State Assembly elections in quick succession. The future looked bleak. "The period of 1985-86 was quite a demoralising phase for us," a veteran leader who is not active in the BJP now had said to me.

On 4 April 1986, Shivraj, oblivious to the challenges before the state leadership in the wake of big defeats, launched a 46-day long Jan-Jagran Yatra from Salkanpur in Raisen district. His *padyatra* made its way through jungles, tribal areas and backward regions and was aimed at raising awareness among the poor. A large number of

## 16 *Shivraj Singh And Rise Of Madhya Pradesh*

people followed him till Budni where the *yatra* culminated into a big gathering. The fear among people there of the forest ranger and other officials was considerably lessened by this *padyatra*. Shivraj shouted at the people, while wielding a *lathi* in his hand, to rise against corrupt forest officials and others oppressing them. At Nasrulla Ganj he organised a big demonstration that sent shockwaves all over. It was during this *padyatra* that he earned the name *pav-pav wale bhaiyya* (a foot soldier) that got changed to *Mama* (maternal uncle) after he launched several schemes to save the girl child in MP, as the Chief Minister.

As days passed by and things progressed on the party front, he was first made the general secretary of the BJYM, and then in 1988 the Madhya Pradesh president, taking over the baton from Vijayendra Singh Sisodiya. He energised the *morcha* and injected new enthusiasm into the workers.

The stint at the helm of the party's youth wing—BJYM—was yet another milestone in his political journey and from here Shivraj never looked back. Arjun Singh had by then returned as the Chief Minister for the second time in MP succeeding Motilal Vora.

The hard worker that Shivraj is, he announced the launch of eight *yatras* simultaneously from as diverse places as Javad in Neemuch district and Dantewada in Bastar on Odisha and Andhra Pradesh borders and from Gwalior, Raigad, Bhabhara in Alirajpur and so on. The three-month-long *yatras* of the youth demanding employment opportunities from the government created an anti-government wave and were a big hit. The Mashal Yatras peaked in their popularity when they reached Bhopal on 7 October 1988. "As many as 1.13 lakh youth courted arrests and the police officials got exhausted writing each name in the diary and doing other formalities...they wanted us to leave but we were hell bent on courting arrests," Shivraj recently told me.

These successful *yatras* from different directions that descended upon Bhopal vaulted him to the top and he became the unchallenged youth leader of the state within no time. It was at this time he got feelers from Arjun Singh to join the Congress 'within a month'. Little did Arjun Singh know about Shivraj's deep anti-Congress feelings which kept on growing in later years as he went on gaining political height in the BJP.

But his best was yet to come. The party nominated him from Budni, a constituency which had been bagged by the Congress in two consecutive elections (1980 and 1985). Shivraj's image as a *pav-pav wale bhaiyya,* his hard work as BJYM's state chief, all came to his help as he humbled Congress candidate Hari Singh and brought back the seat into the BJP fold. That was his first election and first victory. He became an MLA. Chouhan got 43,948 votes and Hari Singh got 21,138—a margin of 22,000-plus votes. His maiden entry into the Assembly was with a bang. The BJP that year formed the government in MP for the second time in history, only to be dismissed in December 1992. Sunderlal Patwa was the CM during the short term.

Between his assuming the new role of first-time MLA and the government's sacking by Delhi, there was a Lok Sabha election in 1991 which Atal Bihari Vajpayee fought from Lucknow and from Vidisha, considered a safe seat. Shivraj again got a chance to work in the field—his first love. Vajpayee secured 58.81% votes without much campaigning there and defeated Congress's Pratap Bhanu Sharma, a local candidate. Shivraj worked very diligently in this election, only to succeed Atalji who forsook Vidisha in favour of Uttar Pradesh's capital.

The party then nominated Shivraj to contest the by-poll after Vajpayee's resignation; this he won handsomely.

From an MLA to an MP within a year or so...his political transition was fast. An orator par excellence, he got numerous opportunities to display his prowess in the Indian Parliament. The first opportunity came after the dismissal of the BJP governments in MP and other states in the wake of Babri demolition, December 1992. Indore's MP, Sumitra Mahajan, recalls how he had launched a scathing attack on the Narasimha Rao government on the dismissal issue and earned a name for himself as a good parliamentarian. There were many more such speeches that followed in his long career in the Lok Sabha. But Shivraj personally remained a low-profile MP and also did not dabble much in the state politics.

He tried to settle down in Delhi but Delhi was not his cup of tea. The politics of intrigue and the high-class society of the elite did not meet with his approval. It was destined that he stay in Delhi for over 15 years as he continued to contest and conquer the Vidisha seat until he became the Chief Minister in November 2005.

I must mention an important incident here that gave yet another twist to his political life.

As a young man, he fought the state BJP president's election against Vikram Verma, a much senior and respectable party leader. While Verma was the party's official candidate, Shivraj had the tacit support and blessings of Sunderlal Patwa, a fact few people knew then. Verma, a former ABVP leader, never got along well with Patwa and hence he was challenged through Shivraj, then a novice.

The BJP, like most other political parties, is a party which does not much favour elections but in the name of intra-party democracy, as history tells us, elections have taken place in many state units all over the country. Shivraj, encouraged by his youth brigade, challenged the party bosses and fought elections going against the party line, in July 2000. When he announced his intention to enter the fray, not many took the young man in his late 40s, seriously. There was a reason for it—Shivraj was a disciplined and unambitious leader, at least overtly. Vikram Verma had the blessings of all top leaders, including Kailash Joshi, Khandelwal and Thakre when the latter was the national president. Yet Shivraj decided to challenge Verma. It was the year when a few months down the line the state was being hived off. Chhattisgarh was to be a reality in November. Incumbent president Nandkumar Sai, a tribal, was set to go over to the new state.

Shivraj, on the advice of some party seniors, went to Delhi and spoke with Thakre to explain his reasons and compulsions why he was contesting. He wanted to bring about 'many changes' in the party. He had also expected guidance from Thakre but Thakre did not say anything nor did he stop him from contesting. The election became inevitable. Vikram Verma, still nursing his injuries from the loss he had suffered in the 1998 Assembly elections, won the organisational polls hands down. Verma was a front-runner for the post of chief ministership if the BJP had managed to conquer the Congress but Digvijay Singh became the Chief Minister once again with a handsome victory. BJP had witnessed infighting...Patwa was dreaming to be CM all over again in 1998; stories did the rounds that it was the veteran leader who engineered Verma's defeat in Dhar with the support of Congress leaders to eliminate future competition for the top slot. There is a section of the party which still believes that Thakre wanted to indirectly teach a lesson to an ambitious Patwa, once very close to him.

The young Turks in the BJP trying to challenge the establishment included Brij Mohan Agarwal (now a powerful minister in Chhattisgarh and 'a-CM-in-waiting'), Prem Prakash Pande, Kailash Vijayvargiya and Narendra Singh Tomar. They all backed Shivraj at

## 20 *Shivraj Singh And Rise Of Madhya Pradesh*

a meeting held in Delhi in the first week of July 2000; he entered the fray only to lose face. This created some tension in his relations with his seniors, including Thakre, who had seen in him as a disciplined party worker. That image got tarnished to some extent.

Did Shivraj feel embittered later? To a certain degree, yes. He was also hugely disappointed and worried about his political future within the party. For the first time he may have realised that 'success has many fathers but failure is an orphan.' That was his first major loss in any election. Though he was not sidelined nor was he treated as an outcast in the party immediately after contesting the election, this defeat set him thinking seriously about himself. A person who would otherwise shy away from parliamentary committee tours to different states, he chose to join one to get out of the depression that had engulfed him at that stage.

He went to Kolkata with the parliamentary committee members on a kind of 'feel-good' tour. In Delhi, Kushabhau Thakre's two-year term as BJP president was over. Bangaru Laxman, a Dalit leader from Andhra Pradesh, was brought in place of Thakre in Delhi. Soon after reaching the helm of party affairs, among the first things that Bangaru did was to call up Shivraj who was in Kolkata. He was asked to leave his tour midway and meet him in Delhi the next day.

Confused, Shivraj developed cold feet. He had just challenged the party line in his home state and had contested elections against the wishes of the party. Thakre had a large heart and had let him off the hook but would Bangaru Laxman do so? Why was he called so urgently? What was in store for him? He spoke to some of his close friends about the summons from the party's new boss. Several questions bombarded his mind.

Yet Shivraj had little choice but to make an air dash to Delhi and call on the party's new boss. He took the next morning flight and reached the party office at 11, Ashoka Road, quietly. He was ushered into Bangaru Laxman's cabin. Laxman straight away broached the subject and offered him the Bhartiya Janata Yuva Morcha's (BJYM) all-India presidentship. Shivraj was swept off his feet.

Flabbergasted… overjoyed? He just did not know how to react for a few moments. Was some dirty politics being played with him or was it a genuine offer? Picking up courage he murmured, "I am a dissident, I have just fought the election for the post of state president in my home state… how can I?"

Bangaru just smiled.

He perhaps wanted his man in Delhi, the one who could challenge people in high places if the situation arose. Did Bangaru think he had plucked an anti-Thakre man to include in his camp? Neither Bangaru (deceased now) nor Shivraj ever knew how he was picked for the national responsibility. But clearly, Shivraj was not a person who would encourage groupism or be used by anyone. The party election was a stand-alone case in his career of some 'indiscipline'. Politically speaking, it was not as if he had violated the party constitution or done anything that could be dubbed as anti-party activity. A cabinet minister once shared with me that "even during a one-to-one-talk he avoids backbiting or scheming against anyone; I think this is his basic nature".

BJYM top post was yet another challenge; and challenges he always liked to accept. He wanted to energise the BJYM at the national level and quickly got down to work. Among many other programmes for the youth, he held a historic youth convention, after criss-crossing the entire country to bring in delegates, at Agra. The convention on 13-14 October, 2000 was marred by heavy unseasonal rains that uprooted large number of make-shift tents and created all-round chaos. But Shivraj remained unruffled and went on to set new standards in organising big youth gatherings. Both Atal Bihari Vajpayee and Advani, the two leaders he adored, came to Agra and praised Shivraj's hard work. Both were impressed with the mammoth gathering and the meticulousness of the organiser.

It was yet another feather in his cap. Shivraj, after a hiccup, was again progressing as a leader. One more significant incident took place in the meanwhile, which unfolds another aspect of Shivraj's nature. Thakre took ill after he had demitted his office. On medical grounds he was advised a month's bed rest. Of the many places in Delhi, he chose to go over to Shivraj's house in Delhi where, along with his wife Sadhana, Shivraj took utmost care of his guru. Both had buried the unpleasant memories of the past.

Bangaru Laxman had to leave the BJP presidentship for alleged corruption of ₹ 1 lakh in the Tehelka sting operation (Operation West End) case and had to resign in 2001. Later he was jailed for the crime.

Shivraj was already on top of the world—a youth leader of the country.

ରାରାରା

Chapter - 3

# THE UMA BHARTI FACTOR

In the eight years that Shivraj has reigned supreme in MP, he has won the hearts of a large number of people but at the same time also given heartbreaks to many. Among these are some party leaders who may possibly stake their claim for the top job some day. Uma Bharti is foremost among them. After the former chief minister's return to the party and becoming an important member of Rajnath Singh's all-India team, Shivraj Singh would not like to take any chances. Since she was denied a second shot at the chief ministership in MP, she is angry with Shivraj but does not show it openly. She is not the one who, if given a chance, would forgive him easily.

Interestingly, when she was contesting elections from UP's Charkhari seat in the Mahoba district in 2012, a couple of Madhya Pradesh ministers were busy trying their best to help her bag the seat. Besides the other 'assistance' that they may have extended for the polls, they had also gone to the extent of trying to influence one of the Election Commission observers, who was from MP, to go out of the way to help Uma. The observer, known for independence and toughness, however, refused to oblige but Uma comfortably won the Lodh-dominated constituency from Bundelkhand and entered the hallowed precincts of the Uttar Pradesh Assembly.

One of the ministers—from the Chambal region—belonged to her camp and genuinely wanted her to win and come back into the mainstream politics, after her recent entry into the BJP (June 2011), courtesy Nitin Gadkari, the then party president. There were reports (*Akhilesh Yadav: Winds of Change* by Sunita Aron) that the 'imported leader' from MP was being projected as the CM—despite protests from the local politicians of UP. It was from Uttar Pradesh that the Ram Janmabhoomi agitation had been launched in the late '80s and where the Ram Temple agitation fire was still burning though at a low ebb. The other minister, a very astute politician of MP, was once very close to Uma as a member of her Cabinet. Later he switched his loyalties and his ambitions grew. He was seen as a challenger to Shivraj from time to time and perhaps made attempts to eliminate at least one contender, should there be an opportune time to dislodge Shivraj Singh during the political uncertainties leading to Assembly elections over the next year. There was always a lurking fear in the minds of many BJP leaders that Uma, having rejoined the BJP after six years in wilderness, might return to MP and make things difficult for them. So the minister wanted her to stay away from MP and keep herself busy in Charkhari.

But nothing of that sort happened as a politically suave Shivraj was made the chief ministerial candidate by the party high command, considering his growing popularity across MP. He then did not give any chance to his critics and political adversaries by spearheading the BJP to its third successive and major victory a year later in November 2013. In the same polls, the other minister lost badly.

But 'firebrand' and 'unpredictable' Uma Bharti continued to maintain her following in her home state. Upon entering the BJP, with lots of backing from the RSS, she won from UP and then was inducted as a vice-president in Rajnath Singh's team. Naturally, her importance in her home state grew, much to the discomfiture of Shivraj, who was instrumental in delaying her entry into the party. To a great extent he succeeded too. And when she actually returned to the party fold, Shivraj could extract a promise from the party high command that she would not be allowed to meddle in the affairs of Madhya Pradesh. During the six years that she was out of the BJP, with his good work, he had won many of her staunch supporters over to his side. Nonetheless, he is always alert about her moves and machinations.

While she grew in stature as a national leader during the Ram Mandir agitation of the Vishwa Hindu Parishad, the RSS and the BJP, she could not retain her standing because of her ill-temper and frequent mood swings. She had to pay the political price for her tempestuousness. Many in the BJP term Uma as her own worst enemy.

Her group of followers and that of her foes almost matched each other in number at one point of time. Today, the opponents have outnumbered her acolytes.

The saffron-clad *sadhvi* was among the few abiding faces of the Ram Janmabhoomi movement of the late '80s and '90s. Her popularity skyrocketed amidst the frenzy that followed the Babri Masjid demolition in Ayodhya on 6 December 1992. As an MP and a prominent *'karsevak'* (volunteer) from Madhya Pradesh, she was present on that eventful day at Ayodhya, on the high stage made for BJP and RSS leaders. There was LK Advani, VHP's Ashok Singhal, Murli Manohar Joshi and Rajamata Vijayaraje Scindia— Uma Bharti's political and spiritual patron, if not the guru. It was said that as chaos grew in Ayodhya, Advani had personally asked Pramod Mahajan and Uma Bharti to go into the unruly gathering and dissuade the slogan-shouting *karsevakas* from damaging the structure. Obviously, Uma and Mahajan could do little in the madding crowd and minutes later the structure was reduced to a massive heap of debris. Clearly, no one was listening to anyone in Ayodhya at that point of time. After the centuries-old structure was brought down, Uma, however, went on record (like many other Hindu leaders, including Balasaheb Thackeray of the Shiv Sena and others in the BJP) stating that she did not have any regrets for the way the mosque was demolished by hundreds of *karsevaks* from the Hindu organisations. Many had gone there from Madhya Pradesh too.

From here onwards she kept building up her image as a Hindu zealot and won the Lok Sabha elections in 1996, 1998 and then in 1999.

Despite being from the backward Bundelkhand's Tikamgarh district, she gambled to shift to Bhopal in 1999 when the Ram Janmabhoomi agitation had lost much of its fervour. She captured Bhopal's parliamentary seat defeating local candidate Suresh Pachauri, then a Rajya Sabha member from the Congress and close to Sonia Gandhi, by 1,68,864 votes in 1999. She polled 55.08% votes as against her rival's 37.79% votes. Shivraj won the same election from the adjacent constituency of Vidisha, winning the seat for the fourth consecutive time with about the same percentage of votes—55.65%.

Before the Bhopal election, Uma had successfully contested the Khajuraho Lok Sabha constituency four times in a row—1989, '91, '96 and '98. When she dumped Khajuraho in favour of Bhopal, Satyavrat Chaturvedi of the Congress, now the AICC spokesman and Rajya Sabha member, won it in 1999.

After the saffron-clad *sadhvi* was inducted into the Cabinet by Atal Bihari Vajpayee, following her emphatic win from Bhopal— where a sizeable number of Muslims live—her ambitions truly started

The Uma Bharti Factor    27

getting the better of her. It was after this significant victory, many party insiders feel, she thought she had the chief minister's chair well within her reach. Some party leaders also argue that her decision of shifting to Bhopal was taken with an eye on the 2003 elections to the State Assembly. By that time she was close to Advani who was calling most of the shots in the party, though the party's national president was Kushabhau Thakre (1998-2000) from MP.

Bharti, along with other leaders like Sushma Swaraj and Pramod Mahajan, was among the team of planners of Advani's Swarna Jayanti Yatra of 1997. Advani is reported to have declared then that Uma Bharti was among the BJP's leaders of the future. She was then in her late 30s. The political significance of Advani's *yatra* was that during this time (May-July,1997) he had urged the Indian Muslims to understand their Hindu brethren's 'cultural nationalism', while passing through Bhopal.

Uma's big political moment came sooner rather than later. It was LK Advani, the Deputy Prime Minister, along with Venkaiah Naidu, BJP president, who made her the chief ministerial candidate and declared it at a rally in Bhopal's Lal Parade ground a few months ahead of the November 2003 polls. She had started an awareness rally against the Congress government from a *Hanuman mandir* (temple) of the small Jam Sawli village in the backward Chhindwara district (represented by Kamal Nath, the Congress leader for a long time.) I was also present there. The rally had culminated at Bhopal where the clarion call to defeat the Congress was given. She was a three-in-one leader to challenge Digvijay Singh. A woman, from the OBC background and a vocal votary of the Hindu cause—indeed a lethal political weapon, against an upper caste Thakur who was struggling to neutralise the anti-incumbency factor against his government. Though Digvijay Singh tried to send out a message of a confident

## 28   Shivraj Singh And Rise Of Madhya Pradesh

winner, the BJP's 'Mr Bantadhar' campaign, snowballed by the fiery oratory of Uma Bharti, hit him where it hurt the most. That the Congress was swept away to its history's lowest two-digit number (38) has been mentioned in another chapter.

But Uma, after taking over as the CM, soon became controversial due to one reason or another. Her poor education (she was a 6th standard drop out from school) was never an impediment in her running of the government. Some people regard her as an intelligent but highly temperamental politician. She speaks good English, has a deep understanding of the Hindu scriptures, history and culture. She is well read too. As a street smart leader, yes, she was a great success but as the chief minister she failed, notwithstanding her experience as a Union minister in several departments under Vajpayee. Her nephews, Rahul and Siddharth and brother, Swami Lodhi, started creating problems for her. Digvijay Singh used to call it her own personal RSS—Rahul, Siddharth and Swami. Corruption charges flew thick and fast as collectors' postings were being decided on the basis of moneybags rather than merit.

As a chief minister, she would stop her car abruptly anywhere on the road in Bhopal if a cow was sighted and would get down briskly to chase the sacred animal to offer her a *roti* (Indian bread), throwing security to the wind, not to talk of the traffic. Press photographers and journalists in Bhopal were a jubilant lot as they would get a good copy and newsy photos more frequently than ever before. Did someone say good governance? Well, that did not seem to be her forte.

During her short tenure as the CM, Kailash Joshi was the party president and many times he differed seriously with her opinions and style of functioning. Once Joshi, a former CM, complained about her to the party's senior leaders in Delhi. I got wind of it and spoke to him as he was boarding the night train to Bhopal. He gave me a truthful account of what he had told the party bosses about Bhopal and did not say not to quote him. My story appeared the next day in *Hindustan Times* where I was working then. I learnt later that a furious Uma Bharti tried to seek an explanation from the party president, a person her father's age, on how the 'damaging story' had appeared in the paper and that he should contradict the same as the party matter was internal and confidential. But Kailash Joshi (among the most honest and straightforward politicians in the BJP in MP) admitted in the meeting with her and other office-bearers at the party headquarters in Bhopal that he had indeed spoken with me of what he had told the party bigwigs in Delhi, and that there was nothing wrong in what he had told me and what had appeared in the newspaper. He refused to issue any rebuttal which left the CM fuming and fretting.

During the 2004 Lok Sabha elections, she as CM had gone to canvass in Shivraj Singh's Vidisha constituency and I had to accompany her in her car. Shivraj was picked up on the way and sat in the front seat of the Ambassador while we were both in the rear seat. I got an opportunity to observe Shivraj closely during the day-long campaigning. He was quiet and mild-mannered; he gave her full respect as the CM. Both are incidentally born in the same year—1959. Uma was on her own trip and kept talking throughout. They offered me a study in contrast. After two-three election meetings we went to Bandrabhan, a small religious place on the banks of the sacred Narmada river near Shahganj. There she took a dip in the river, bathed and worshipped at a small temple across the river atop a hillock while the others and I waited for her. I saw a CM, very devoutly religious and sincere in performing her religious rituals despite Lok Sabha campaigning pressures.

## Shivraj Singh And Rise Of Madhya Pradesh

She appeared to have normal, cordial relations with Shivraj, who was a long-standing MP, and a former national president of the Bhartiya Janata Yuva Morcha (BJYM). Later their relations soured to the extent that she started hating Shivraj; people say she still does. Shivraj, as is his wont, avoids any direct confrontation with her.

## The Foiled Bid

The story of her foiled bid to become CM after Babulal Gaur in 2005 is very absorbing. It was also a blessing in disguise for Shivraj who became the CM, partly because she failed to play adroitly whatever cards she had, and partly because she had just come out of her suspension and the leaders in Delhi (whom she had accused during a party meeting which was telecast live) were still deeply hurt. They included Pramod Mahajan, Arun Jaitley and Venkaiah Naidu. In her outburst she had not even spared Advani and therefore she invited her short-lived suspension.

Her erratic working in the government earlier had started proving to be a headache for the party's senior leaders in Delhi and Bhopal all over again. The media was quite happy as it was getting stories after stories about the continued antics of Uma and her relatives. Bureaucrats were a scared lot as she would shout at anyone under any pretext. She changed a chief secretary just because her religious guru told her not to see a man with a squint in the morning, a fact she had shared with me after exiting her office. The Chief Secretary, AV Singh, did have a small defect in one of his eyes and that became the reason of his ouster, though she had flown him to Maheshwar in her chopper moments after her grand and pompous swearing-in ceremony at the Lal Parade ground. Uma's swearing-in clearly did not gel with the façade of a *sadhvi*. But that was Uma Bharti—sometimes *sadhvi*, sometimes politician and

The Uma Bharti Factor    31

sometimes both. Truly an enigmatic personality!

Soon after she took over as the CM, the english magazine *India Today* had commented on 15 December 2003: "In the wreckage of Digvijay Singh's defeat lies a terrible truth: If politics is about delivering intangibles then one of Congress's pin-up CMs has failed to do just that. With no tangible development to couch the anti-incumbency, 'Shreeman Bantadhar' (Mr Failure) had no answers for the lack of power, roads and employment. His social engineering, decentralisation of power and literacy campaigns had the hollow shrill of a broken conch. BJP's Uma Bharti, a mass leader and public performer, had to do nothing but be herself: Honest, assertive, unpurchasable and mesmerising on the street."

The negative feedback of her governance made her very upset, very often and that led to more faux pas. The BJP in Delhi was awaiting the right moment to remove her because public perception was building up that the party's first woman chief minister was damaging BJP's image and providing no hope after Digvijay's hopeless rule.

On 18 August 2004 afternoon, she suddenly called for Babulal Gaur, one of her senior Cabinet colleagues, and asked him to immediately go to Delhi—by train—to attend former president Shankar Dayal Sharma's birth anniversary celebration on 19 August where the new Prime Minister, Dr Manmohan Singh, Sonia Gandhi, ex-Prime Minister Atal Bihari Vajpayee and Ex Deputy PM, LK Advani were also invited. Uma apparently wanted to avoid meeting Sonia Gandhi what with her diatribes against 'the lady of Italian origin' in the poll campaigns that year. Sharma was from Bhopal and was the chief minister of Bhopal State which was merged in the later-day MP. Gaur reached Delhi in the morning by the Bhopal-Nizamuddin Inter-City Express (he was denied the state plane) and around 6 pm he went to the anniversary function at 'Karma Bhoomi' near Raj Ghat. There he saw a vacant chair next to Advani. He occupied it. Soon the PM and other dignitaries arrived and the *bhajan* singing began. As the brief function progressed to its end, Advani asked him when he would return to Bhopal to which Gaur, the then home minister, replied 'tonight by train'. Advani reportedly asked him to see him at night and put off his return journey. As Babulal Gaur reached his home, Advani showed him some clippings of newspapers saying that CM Uma's brother Swami Lodhi had threatened to sit on a *dharna* against a few corrupt ministers in her Cabinet. "This is damaging the image of the BJP government and you try to counsel her to change her way of working," Advani reportedly told Babulal to which Babulal replied that it was beyond his capacity to do that. Advani then asked him to go to Vajpayee who too repeated the same thing. He shared with him the party's concern about the goings-on in Madhya Pradesh. Here too (according to Babulal Gaur), he said he was helpless and couldn't bring about the change in his chief minister. He returned to Bhopal on 21 August, 2004. As luck (bad luck for Uma) would have it, the Hubli (Karnataka) court verdict went against her in the Indian Tricolour dishonour case and the court issued a non-bailable warrant against her. There was no need for her to resign dramatically as various legal options were open to her then. But fickle-minded as she was, she threw away her hard-earned chief ministership, little realising that in politics it is not so easy to get back to the high chair.

The party, already fed up with her erratic functioning, jumped at the opportunity and quickly advised her to resign, with a clear plan in mind not to install her again. But she put forth a condition before quitting: "Make my man the CM." Considering the fluid political situation, the party had to concede to her demand that her successor would be of her choice and not of the party. She anointed Babulal Gaur, a seemingly unambitious veteran politician who was Bhopal-centric. A very senior BJP leader told me that she took Gaur to her Shyamla Hills official bungalow and made him take an oath in the small, make-shift temple she had set up soon after she became the CM. Babulal also took an 'oath' that once she was set free from the court case and back in Bhopal he would, without a murmur, make place for her. In a way he was keeping the seat warm for her. "Honestly, I had never thought that I would be the CM ever because it was Uma who was out to cut my ticket from Bhopal in 2003 and due to party's senior leaders' intervention I managed to get one then," Babulal had told me soon after becoming the CM.

When Uma got entangled in the court case, the party leaders had different plans up their sleeves. BJP leaders actually wanted Shivraj to be made the CM then itself because they knew the limitations of Gaur, who had no pan-Madhya Pradesh presence, not to speak of great winning appeal. Also, changing CMs frequently, without any ostensible reason, would have tarnished their image and eroded the newly-earned base of the BJP. A senior leader confided in me that to pacify Uma, they had to appoint a CM of her choice and Gaur got his name entered in MP's political history for ever.

The CM's post came to him like a lottery. Babulal stayed as Chief Minister for 15 months—August 2004-November 2005, courtesy Uma Bharti but also quit it at a very short notice. I was with Gaur in Indore attending a marriage the day he got a call from LK Advani asking him to resign. Gaur told me quite matter-of-factly: "I told Advaniji that I am in Indore and will go back to Bhopal tomorrow and put in my papers." But Advani asked him not to make a hasty decision and wait for the party's signal. After the call from Delhi, which his PA Santosh Sharma had received in the late afternoon

## 34 Shivraj Singh And Rise Of Madhya Pradesh

when he was attending an *arti* at *Sadhvi* Ritumbhara's religious function, he called back Advani and told him that after attending the wedding reception, he would return to Bhopal the next day. He resigned three days later but not before proposing Shivraj Singh's name at the legislature party meeting. Uma was furious with him for letting her down and not sticking to the oath. In return for giving up the chief ministership without creating any ruckus and giving headaches to the party, Vajpayee and Advani asked him what he would like to be—a party president (which Shivraj was then), or a Rajya Sabha member, Assembly Speaker or a senior minister. He chose the last option and was sworn in as minister of industries and commerce in Shivraj Singh's Cabinet immediately. He continues to be a minister till date with the politically significant home portfolio.

For Shivraj, it was not easy to become the CM as most MLAs belonged to Uma Bharti. She had not only threatened to break the party but had created all kinds of scenes in front of the central observers—Rajnath Singh, Arun Jaitley and the all-powerful Pramod Mahajan. She had reportedly spoken to 20-25 MLAs at her Civil Lines bungalow that day, ready to go to any extent, even as the legislature party meeting began at the party headquarters. The situation became volatile; some of those attending the meeting suggested that she be made the CM again and tried to propose her name after Babulal had already proposed Shivraj's name. A few MLAs raised their voices in her support. Sumitra Mahajan, a veteran MP, called up Pralhad Patel, Uma's top supporter, at the last moment seeking help to avert an unpleasant situation. She requested that Uma go with the party line but to no avail. The party's top leaders had decided on Shivraj. As the MLAs from her camp got wind of the high command's clear intentions of making Shivraj the chief minister, she entered the hall, delivered a speech, tried her best to

The Uma Bharti Factor    35

change the situation in her favour, shouted at senior leaders and stormed out of the hall accusing Jaitley and Mahajan of stabbing her in the back.

As a reaction, outside the BJP office, Uma's supporters vandalised vehicles shouting slogans like "*lathi-goli khayenge, Umaji ko layenge* (We will suffer beating and bullets but will bring Uma back); *ghar-ghar ki beti kaisi ho, Uma Bharti jaisi ho* (how should our daughters be, they should be like Uma Bharti)." They also shouted slogans against the two party leaders, especially Mahajan, who was widely seen as the strongest supporter of Shivraj. There was a skirmish between the two groups of the party. Workers came to blows and the police had a tough time controlling them as tension mounted outside the office.

The transfer of power in MP was anything but smooth.

Inside the hall, strategist Mahajan, the then mighty national general secretary of the BJP, with the help of Arun Jaitley and others, managed to install his own man as the 18th CM of MP. When asked by the media 'why Shivraj?', a smiling Mahajan, I vividly recall, told a press conference in a lighter vein, *"Shivraj ka sasural (Gondia) Maharashtra mein hai aur main bhi Maharashtra ka hun isliye inhe chuna"* (Shivraj's wife belongs to Maharashtra and I am also from Maharashtra, so I have chosen him).

As Shivraj was trying to relish his moment of glory, Uma was once again on the streets, launching 'Ram Roti Padyatra' from Bhopal to Ayodhya in protest and announcing that Bhopal's battle would be fought in Delhi. Hours later, she was expelled from the BJP for the second time within a year.

On 30 April 2006, she formed her own party Bhartiya Jan Shakti (BJS) at Ujjain, an ancient religious town. She went inside the famous Lord Shiva's Mahakaal Temple's *grabha griha* (sanctum sanctorum) along with Raghunandan Sharma and former Delhi CM Madanlal Khurana to offer the party flag to the God, as a symbolic launch of her party. Later she addressed a public meeting at Tower Chouraha in Ujjain and declared the formal launch of the party amidst roaring applause from the crowd and also announced her intention to fight against Shivraj's BJP. The BJS fought elections separately in MP in 2008 from 220 seats or so. She herself stood from her home district Tikamgarh but lost to Yadvendra Singh Bundela of the Congress and only five candidates of her party (BJS) could win while the Uttar Pradesh-based Bahujan Samaj Party (BSP) of Mayawati sent seven candidates to the Assembly that year. BJP candidate Akhand Pratap Singh's deposit was forfeited at Tikamgarh as he finished a poor third behind Uma. Shivraj had returned to power as a much stronger Chief Minister having won the poll on his own winning 143 seats, against Congress's 71. Uma was a spent bullet, as it seemed then.

Now that she is back in the BJP and an MLA from UP, her heart still 'bleeds' for MP.

ଔଔଔଔ

Chapter - 4

# TREADING CAUTIOUSLY

On 29 November 2005, soon after the low-key swearing-in ceremony at the Raj Bhawan was over and after chatting with the Governor, Dr Balram Jhakhar, his old friend and the former Lok Sabha Speaker, LK Advani was informally telling a group of senior ministers: "*Shivraj ko jo bhi kam party ne jab-jab diya unhone achha hi kar ke dikhaya hai; woh gambhir hain aur imandar bhi...yeh naya daitava bhi ve bakhubhi nibhayenge*" (Whenever Shivraj has been given a particular task or responsibility by the party, he has carried it out well; he is sincere and honest... he will ably shoulder the new responsibility).

Advaniji, Atalji and Jaswant Singh were among those prominent leaders who had come for the oath-taking ceremony of their party's Madhya Pradesh unit president who was, after much drama by Uma Bharti and her supporters, installed as the third BJP Chief Minister in about two years.

A political issue was being made out of it by the Congress Party, though much reduced in the State Assembly, charging that the BJP did not know how to rule the state and that it was taking the people for granted. First, Uma Bharti resigned and now Babulal Gaur was suddenly removed. (The Congress leader-turned Governor,

## 38 Shivraj Singh And Rise Of Madhya Pradesh

Dr Jhakhar, had curiously asked Vajpayee and Advani over a cup of tea at the Raj Bhawan itself why they had removed Gaur?)

The two quick changes in Bhopal had offered a readymade issue to an otherwise demoralised Congress in the state.

So all eyes were on Shivraj—how would he perform and take the state forward and silence BJP's critics. Those were definitely tense moments for a fledgling Chief Minister. Two big hurdles were firmly placed against him: First, he had little experience of holding any office in the past; he was never a minister or a mayor and had to learn the art of governance in such a big and diverse state. Second, Uma Bharti, after a few months, had set up her own party—Bhartiya Jan Shakti (April 2006) and some of the BJP stalwarts from different areas, such as Raghunandan Sharma, Pralhad Patel, Shailendra Pradhan and many others, had joined her. The *sadhvi* was enemy number one of the government and the CM, stung as she was by the denial of another chance by the party, in place of Babulal Gaur. She spared no opportunity to hit out at Shivraj and his government.

Uma was the rallying point for all the Hindu forces while in the BJP and also after she had been expelled from it. Her mega swearing-in function at the Lal Parade ground had completely painted the city saffron. The huge stage had many *sadhus*, saints and VHP leaders blessing her on the 8 December 2003 function. Earlier, Sunderlal Patwa (1990) too had taken his oath on this very ground—both lasted in office for a short time. But none of the three swearings-in of Shivraj took place on that sprawling ground. Did Shivraj think of it as a bad omen? First he was sworn in at the Raj Bhawan—the traditional place where CMs used to take oaths in earlier decades and his next two oath ceremonies were held amidst large crowds at the Jamboori Maidan and were quite a show of strength.

In December 2013, Shivraj had gained sufficient political clout following the party's third successive and big win and therefore Advani, Modi, Rajnath Singh, Sushma Sawaraj and several chief ministers such as Vasundhara Raje, Raman Singh, former Andhra CM Chandrababu Naidu, as also prominent industrialists Anil Ambani (Reliance), Abhay Firodia (Force Motors), Shashi and Anshuman Ruia (Essar), Rajendra Gupta (Trident), Amit Kalyani (Bharat Forge), Ravi Sharan Sanghi (Sanghi Industries) and Swati Mujumdar (Symbiosis Institute, Pune) were present at the brief oath-taking ceremony. A large number of private planes and choppers had descended upon Bhopal for Shivraj for the first time.

Yes, Shivraj was changing fast from a shy state leader into a confident national leader. He was casting his net far and wide.

## A Liberal Hindu

Shivraj has been a devout Hindu. He does not ever leave his house without reciting the *Gayatri Mantra*, something normally the upper-caste Brahmin men do as their religious ritual after their thread ceremony is done—preferably at the age of eight years. They become eligible at that age, as per the ancient Hindu religious practice. But despite his religious bent of mind and a touch of Hindutva, Shivraj never sported saffron attire like Uma Bharti nor portrayed his image as a staunch Hindu leader like Narendra Modi or Advani or Uma Bharti. That is a major difference between him and Modi—the two top BJP chief ministers, who are performing well in their respective states and are strengthening the right-wing party in their own way. Yet, Shivraj is not seen as a '*Hindu hriday samrat*' nor does he perhaps want to project his image like that.

Not to speak of wearing saffron robes, Shivraj's sartorial preferences are also very limited—a simple kurta pyjama—the homely dress of rural India and of the middle classes. Despite

40 *Shivraj Singh And Rise Of Madhya Pradesh*

spending close to 15 years in Delhi, people had not seen him in expensive designer *kurtas* or fancy jackets from well-known brands. Nothing has changed about his dressing style over the years. He prefers to look like a common man, but there are no idiosyncrasies, *a la* Lalu Yadav.

When he was made the CM, he was the BJP State unit president for sometime (May 2005 to 27 Feb 2006), a post he had lost five years ago to Vikram Verma in a straight contest. Things were to take a positive turn in his favour as both his defeats catapulted him to bigger positions later—first in the race to state BJP unit chief's post and second in the 2003 State Assembly elections which the party made him fight against Chief Minister Digvijay Singh in Raghogarh.

Minutes after his name was announced by the party's central leadership at Ashoka Road in Delhi, I had met him there late in the evening. He had appeared worried. The next day, on way to Raghogarh, he had stopped in Bhopal and had granted me an exclusive interview for *Hindustan Times* at a common friend Dilip Suryavanshi's house, where he had briefly told me how it had all happened.

When the party asked him to fight an Assembly election, Shivraj was a member of the BJP Parliamentary Board and was hesitant to go to Raghogarh. He told me in a personal conversation that it was Uma Bharti who had proposed his name having been already declared as the CM candidate for the forthcoming elections. Following some discussion on the issue, Atalji, as Prime Minister, had intervened and gesticulated towards him in the meeting and just said two words: "*jao ladho*" (go and fight).

Shivraj's options were closed after Vajpayee, in a way, ordered him to contest. The PM had a special liking for him.

Shivraj's idea of not going to Raghogarh was, in fact, to help the

Treading Cautiously    41

party by moving around in the state and campaigning in various constituencies but the party's strategy was to pin Digvijay Singh down in his pocket borough. Shivraj was an MP from Vidisha, and his loss would not have affected the party much.

Shivraj expectedly lost in Raghogarh with Digvijay securing 58,233 votes and Shivraj 37,067 votes. Paradoxically, Digivijay won his own *garh* (fort) but the Congress under his leadership lost power in the whole state—for straight 15 years from that day.

Within two years destiny brought Shivraj Singh to the high chair in MP. He contested the by-election to enter the Assembly from Budni constituency which he had won once in 1990 but could not complete the term as he was sent to succeed Atal Bihari Vajpayee from Vidisha Lok Sabha constituency. In Budni he had given a slogan '*ek note, ek vote*' (one note, one vote) and won the election hands down. He did not take donations for his election, his election campaigner told me. I had the occasion to cover that election and we had walked many kilometres in his mass voters contact programme in the villages where his popularity remained high.

In 2008 and 2013, he was returned to the Assembly with big margins from Budni. He made history recording the biggest ever victory by any CM—84,805 votes margin. This time around to control the possible damage that ex-finance minister Raghavji Bhai (sacked from the Cabinet and the party for sodomy case) may have caused as the sitting MLA, Shivraj contested from Vidisha and Budni, winning both seats, only to vacate Vidisha. In Vidisha his margin was much less—16,996—than Budni because local people felt that there was no permanent representative who cared for Vidisha. They knew before going to vote that he would vacate the seat in favour of Budni, which happened within a week. Though Shivraj had declared in 2008 he would make Vidisha (population

## 42 Shivraj Singh And Rise Of Madhya Pradesh

less than 1.50 lakh) a modern town, it remains a backward town struggling for basic amenities. In the Lok Sabha, the constituency was once represented by Jan Sangh's Ramnath Goenka (owner of Indian Express Group) who did not look back even once after winning. Then came Vajpayee who also won and quit the seat and after Shivraj quit it in 2006, Sushma Swaraj is the local MP, though she is not from Madhya Pradesh. She was however first elected unopposed to the Rajya Sabha from MP in March 2006, along with Arjun Singh and Vikram Verma, among others.

Sushma, the Leader of the Opposition in the Lok Sabha, when asked about the continued backwardness of the constituency, said she had brought a Central Government diesel engine parts manufacturing plant there and had fought for it with the then Railway Minister, Mamata Banerjee. However, land selection and acquisition has not started yet, even after two years, according to local residents. Sushma says more road network is also being laid from Bina onwards to help attract new industries to Vidisha.

Shivraj's three years in power from 2005-2008 were full of activity but unlike Uma he did not throw any tantrums; instead he got down to work seriously from day one. "I wanted to utilize each and every minute," he had told me then. His holding of the unique panchayats at the CM house had begun in 2006 as a tool of effective and unique governance practice and continues to help him get closer to people to know their problems.

But solving of people's issues through panchayats was not sufficient for Shivraj. Problems kept darting at him from unexpected quarters. The most shocking and challenging was the daylight murder of a professor in Ujjain. Prof HS Sabharwal of the famous Madhav College was allegedly attacked and killed (October 2006) by students linked to the ABVP. More than 20 student leaders were jailed and the incident hogged national headlines, much to the chagrin of the BJP Government in Bhopal, and the Chief Minister. Shivraj was himself an ABVP leader of his times. He was shell-shocked. The case dragged on for many months as the slain professor's son, Himanshu Sabharwal, approached the Supreme Court and pleaded that he did not expect to get justice in Madhya Pradesh so the case be shifted out of MP. The Supreme Court agreed and the case was transferred and tried in Nagpur High Court. Ultimately, all the student leaders were set free and the Government was saved from ignominy—that of killing a college professor and protecting the killers as they belonged to the party in power.

It was about the same time that BJP MLA and former Minister Dr Gauri Shankar Shejwar (now the Forest Minister) was expelled from the BJP. He was close to Uma Bharti but later returned to the BJP. The Government was, in this particular phase, also grappling with yet another serious problem: dacoit gang Rambabu Gadariya's terror. In the Shivpuri-Gwalior area, he had become a deadly menace for the police force. He was once declared 'dead' by the police but he emerged alive to shock the Government machinery by killing four men of the Gujjar community in Shivpuri (Karera jungles), thus challenging the authority of the Government. But the government succeeded in finally eliminating him and his dreaded gang by April 2007.

It was on 25 August 2008 that Shivraj completed 1,000 days in office, the first non-Congress chief minister to do so in 52 years of MP's political history. Today, when one looks back, the widely celebrated day has paled into insignificance as he kept climbing the ladder of popularity and kept winning elections. Today Shivraj is a kind of a national hero but at that time he was facing multi-faceted challenges from his own former party colleague Uma, as well as the

## 44  *Shivraj Singh And Rise Of Madhya Pradesh*

Congress. It was during this time he had told me in an interview for *Dainik Bhaskar* (25 August 2008) that he was not looking back at history but was staring into the future. "Painting BJP's image of being an anti-poor party was a conspiracy of the Opposition and I needed to change the perception; all my policies are aimed at them (the poor)," he had said.

Shivraj's evolving art of governance was very different. He was talking of inclusive growth for all. He wanted to make Madhya Pradesh a shining state and gave a slogan '*Swarnim* Madhya Pradesh *Banayenge*' (we will make a golden Madhya Pradesh). Perhaps, it was on the lines of the 'Shining India' campaign, though the latter was an election slogan of the NDA under Vajpayee.

For the '*Swarnim* Madhya Pradesh,' he had invoked the people of MP to come forward and do their bit while the government was doing its own work. It was one of his favourite stories which he would often narrate in public meetings initially: "When I would visit any village, a large number of people would turn out to garland me, felicitate me and spend thousands of rupees on my welcome functions and then during the programme they would urge me to sanction *sarkari paisa* (government funds) for cleaning up of a village well or drilling a hand pump or such paltry work…I would then ask why did you spend so much money on my welcome… you could have utilised the same for the well cleaning or digging a new well for the village… but no, they would expect the government to do it for them…this mentality had to be changed in the larger interest of the state." He had repeated the story in a number of public meetings to send out a strong message that communities (also) owed something to the state.

While fulfilling the tasks of the government he had his own way of getting work done. In administration, he started relying on the bureaucrats like his own trusted men to deliver what he wanted; industrialisation had begun in right earnest and road construction had been undertaken in a big way as the base of various physical infrastructure projects. Madhya Pradesh was always known to be a state where roads were almost non-existent and the power scenario was dismal.

Social infrastructure and physical infrastructure were both developed in the state simultaneously and that is where Shivraj gains his height as the tallest Chief Minister in the history of MP. During Digvijay Singh's regime the roads network was in a horrible condition and across the country MP had earned a bad name. Once superstar Amitabh Bachchan visited Indore in mid '90s and had commented on the state of bad roads that he had to travel on. But as has been said elsewhere in the book, infrastructure development was never the priority of the Digvijay Singh regime. Contrastingly, between 2009-2014, roads worth ₹ 20,000 crore have been built by the Public Works Department ( PWD) alone. Principal Secretary PWD, KK Singh, IAS, says that 13,475 km of roads were built new while 12,430 km were repaired and improved. This had multiple advantages as it improved communication between villages and urban centres and also attracted industries and enhanced tourism. In the tourism sector too, the MP Government got many central government awards in 2012 and 2013.

In the health sector much more is actually required to be done to which he also agrees—that IMR and MMR figures are not very encouraging. It was during this time that a massive drug kit purchase fraud worth ₹ 7 crore was exposed. Kits to be purchased under the National Rural Health Mission (NRHM) were fraudulently purchased by Dr Yogiraj Sharma, Health Director, in connivance with many other government officials. It clearly showed the nexus of officers-doctors-suppliers and the massive corruption in the health department. Dr Sharma was suspended following a Lokayukta case and then was terminated from government service. "The health sector continues to be in a bad shape in MP and the Chief Minister needs to seriously look into the entire gamut of health services and medical education scenario in his third term," many in Madhya Pradesh strongly feel.

Shivraj tried to improve the roads, power and agricultural conditions within three years of his rule and registered a big victory in November 2008 polls. Uma Bharti, as BJS chief, had said on completion of Shivraj's 1,000 days in office, in August 2008 that, 'she was unable to see any government or a Chief Minister in MP'. She could not justify her statement as Shivraj stormed back to power to become the CM for the second time with 143 seats in a House of 230.

Many of the Shivraj-watchers underestimate him as a politician of substance. But the glimpses of his leadership skills were far more evident in 2008 than ever before. He had not only started many pro-people schemes but had also understood the mood of people against his own MLAs who were either unpopular or facing corruption charges. Thus 61 sitting MLAs were denied tickets for the 2008 elections and 38 new candidates had won the polls then.

Senior minister, Jayant Malaiya, told me once that his Shivraj's hard work and his unmatched zeal for development is the key to his success. "I have worked under many chief ministers and have held many portfolios like housing and environment, water resources, industries, finance and have seen him conducting Cabinet meetings with great understanding of complex issues…I can say that when I was water resources minister, Shivraj's knowledge of the department was much better than mine," Malaiya confesses. In his new capacity as the finance minister for the past six months or so, he quotes a recent incident when the CM pulled up an IAS officer for her goof-up in GDP and GSDP figures, she showed that they were decreasing in MP, which the CM knew was incorrect. He was to make a speech before the 14th Finance Commission the next day in Bhopal and therefore he took the faux pas seriously, Malaiya confided to me, pointing to the CM's awareness about development statistics.

The credit for bringing the party back to power in 2008 must be given to the Shivraj-Narendra Singh Tomar duo who had worked in tandem to emerge victorious inspite of the challenge from Uma Bharti's BJS. It is already mentioned that Uma's new party could win only five seats and she herself lost on her home turf of Bundelkhand. Shivraj very shrewdly maneuvered to keep the anti-incumbency factor at bay. The same formula and strategy he repeated in 2013 by axing several MLAs and ministers and effectively neturalising the anti-incumbency factor, a strong reason why Sheila Dixit lost in Delhi.

The all-inclusive policies and non-confrontationist approach have become hallmarks of Shivraj Singh and they combined to deliver timely results. According to Yogesh Kumar's edit page piece in *Indian Express* (22.11. 2013), in 2008, the BJP won 25 scheduled caste (reserved) seats out of the total 35 constituencies while the Congress managed to win only nine. And out of 47 tribal reserved constituencies, the BJP had won 28 seats in that election. A separate team of Shivraj worked in 2013 in different villages and brought together small NGOs and social bodies to enhance the voting percentage among the poor and the unorganised, to support the BJP.

"I think when people voted the BJP back to power in 2008 they wanted me to finish the unfinished agenda of developmental works," Shivraj told me recently in connection with this book's research.

48  *Shivraj Singh And Rise Of Madhya Pradesh*

Clearly during his initial days and until 2008, perceptible change was being felt by the people of Madhya Pradesh all across. "People had voted for the continuity of development and had favoured the policies of my government." He had then told me that he would like to work as a CEO of the state with a humanitarian approach.

I still remember the water crisis that loomed large in Madhya Pradesh in 2008. After his victory, on his first day as second-term CM he had addressed the water scarcity issue at a high level meeting and then had visited a few slum areas of the capital to try and know their problems. Bhopal now sees a number of large slum areas converted into low-cost apartments for the slum dwellers so they can live much more decently. Their previous dwellings were full of filth and had squalor around. The dream of making Bhopal a slum-free city is gradually taking solid shape.

In an interview to me, the first to any newspaper after his victory, he had categorically stated that he would try and install separate power feeder lines for domestic and agriculture use and would attempt to make 24×7 power availability (*Dainik Bhaskar* interview dt 10.12.2008). He had also spoken at length about agriculture and had wanted to bring about changes in wheat and gram cultivation in MP. Today, five years down the line, MP is among the largest producers of wheat and gram–dreams that have come true after his consistent efforts and vision. Separate electricity feeder lines have been installed and a minimum of eight hours of uninterrupted quality power is being provided to farmers—promises fulfilled and votes secured. Rakesh Sahani, the then chief secretary and chairman of the now dissolved Madhya Pradesh State Electricity Board (MPSEB), told me that he had begun the initial work on feeder lines in early 2008.

I recall the CM's famous statement from that interview that "*mein garibon ka rakhwala hun*" (I am the guardian of the poor.)

A London-based writer and lecturer in politics, Louise Tillin, had predicted about the 2013 Assembly polls thus: "Electoral outcomes in MP (and Chhattisgarh) will be a verdict on their different welfare models," and that is precisely what happened in both states where the BJP came back to power in 2013—making a rare hat-trick.

Economist Surjit Bhalla on 'politics of welfare' was quoted as saying last year in *Outlook* (30 December, 2013) that "welfarism has not delivered votes historically since the mid-80s… now we have evidence that bad economics, even when perpetuated with welfarism, does not deliver votes." He argued, "Empirical evidence shows that economic performance and growth deliver votes…."

Promises and welfarism remind me of another action of Shivraj which endeared him to the people. During one of his tours to Vindhya Pradesh, people came up with a demand for a separate revenue division of Shahdol, cut-off from the large Rewa division with many districts. He said it would be done within a time frame and gave them the date of setting up the new division. Upon his return to Bhopal he asked the Chief Secretary to start doing necessary work before the deadline. When the revenue division was to be created, a function was organised by the local administration. I had accompanied the CM to Shahdol that day –14 June 2008. At a huge gathering of people, he not only declared that the division was inaugurated, he called the newly-appointed Divisional Commissioner—Arun Tiwari and the Inspector-General of Police, PR Mathur, on the dais, held their hands up in the air and waved to the public saying: "I have physically presented your officers in front of you to believe that what I say, I do."

A similar thing he had done earlier when the Government of India turned down the proposal to change the name of Hoshangabad district to Narmada Puram (it being located on the banks of the sacred river). He created a Narmada Puram Revenue Division, which was well within the jurisdiction of the State Government. There also he presented the civil servants as the Commissioner and IGP before the people.

## Liberal Image, Unique Thoughts

His first challenge was over after the victory of 2008 as a three-year old Chief Minister. During the first three years and the next five years Shivraj somehow managed to stay away from big controversies—political or otherwise. Yes, he was trapped in a 'dumper case' in his early days when some dumpers (open goods carrying trucks) were rented to ferry building materials etc in Jaypee Cement factory in Rewa, owned by Jay Prakash Gaur and his sons, Sunny and Manoj Gaur, in his name. The Congress tried to make capital out of it and made complaints to anti-graft agencies but Shivraj came out clean from what the Congress tried to paint as a scandal. It did trouble him a lot those days as some of the party insiders and ministers too had tried to destabilise him using this 'little scam'.

He did make some political statements from time to time that stuck to him—good or bad; the statements also help us understand his thinking pattern. Just before the Commonwealth Games, when the ceremonial torch passed through Bhopal and the Chief Minister, otherwise a sports lover, was expected to receive it and see it off from the capital, he took a stand: "I will not do it as I feel the Commonwealth Games are passé. We no longer live under the British Queen's regime; the world has changed…Olympic Games, Asian Games are alright but why Commonwealth Games? Why are we being reminded of the yoke of the British empire, all over again?"

He had stayed away from the torch ceremony.

The sports lover that he is, Shivraj was among the first chief ministers to demand Bharat Ratna for the hockey legend (late) Major Dhyanchand. "In days of cricket mania, he stood his ground that before Sachin Tendulkar it was Dhyanchand who merited the topmost civil honour," says his close aide.

SK Rout, Director General of Police (retired) and the one who served three CMs in the key post of Additional Director General (Intelligence), once told me: "Shivraj Singh has great qualities in that he does not waste time on things which are of no interest to him. When you talk to him he won't give you much of facial expressions but his hard disk (mind) keeps working instantly and solves the issue without letting you know if he liked your suggestion or not, or what was the solution to a particular situation. He listens a lot, observes a lot and talks less...only when required." Rout was also all praises for his ability to carry out things with lots of patience despite political urgencies and rivalries. He would wait patiently to do what he thought was best, said the respectable IPS officer who had a good stint in the CBI.

People also recollect Shivraj's other statement made conscientiously that, "Rajya Sabha (the Upper House in Parliament) be abolished because legislators are openly traded by those with money bags." He did not take it much further as the BJP had not liked this but he still feels the same.

He is also a votary of state-funded elections to curb black money. "*Main hamesha chahta hun ki Vidhan Sabha aur Lok Sabha ke elections ek saath ho aur uska kharcha rajya sarkar uthaye; Vidhan Sabha ki samay seema nishchit ho aur uske pehle chunav kisi bhi keemat per na ho isse desh ka jo paisa bachega aur vikas ke kam jyada ho sakenge....* (I have always held that Assembly and Lok Sabha polls should take place together and states should bear the cost; the Assembly can't be dissolved anytime, there should be fixed terms under any situation, so the money saved can be utilised for more development works of the country).

If Shivraj's personality is carefully studied in the past eight years in the high seat of power, one thing appears very prominent: his liberal face. A CM house insider was telling me a few months ago that when Shivraj was discussing the plan to raise the honorarium of all *pundits and pujaris* of the government-run temples (priests who perform religious rituals) in the state, he instantly came up with a suggestion and told his secretary, an IAS officer, that those who performed the same work at the mosques should also be given the same honorarium as the Hindu priests. This underscores the fact that within the four walls of his office he was thinking of the Muslim clergymen's welfare at par with Hindu *Pundits*.

Shivraj shot into national prominence in 2013 when he wore a skull cap at an Eid programme in Bhopal where he would invariably go to greet Muslims. "After all, they are also the citizens of this country," he had argued to me in a conversation, adding, "just by wearing a Muslim *topee*, I don't get converted... yes I am a Hindu and I am proud of it but it's my duty to respect different religions and faiths as a Chief Minister." At the CM house, he organises functions on all major religious festivals and invites everyone—Muslims, Sikhs and Christians. "The house is not my house—it belongs to people of all religions and my gates are always open for them," he says like a typical politician...but only after actually having thrown the gates open to all of them and allowing them to celebrate their main festivals at the CM House with the CM and his family.

Shivraj's wearing the Muslim skull cap came within a few months of Narendra Modi's refusal to do so when a Muslim offered it to him. Thus the stark difference between the two leaders came to the fore, though there is no comparison between the two individuals—

aggressive Modi is already an international star and has overcome all the charges against him. Shivraj is creating a niche for himself slowly but steadily.

Shivraj is very humane, a little shy but a sensitive politician in his approach—a distinctive facet of his nature. Soon after forming his Cabinet in 2008, I had written an analytical piece on his choice of ministers, the portfolios given to them and their backgrounds and had raised some questions. Tukojirao Pawar, a scion of the princely family of Dewas, was higher education minister in 2007-08 but his performance was not up to the mark. There were many complaints against him of all kinds. So I wondered how he was taken back into the Cabinet. At 8 am that day after reading the piece in *Dainik Bhaskar*, Bhopal, Shivraj had called me to explain why Pawar had been inducted into the cabinet and had wanted me to keep the reason confidential. Now after five years, I can tell my readers that since Pawar was seriously ill those days, dropping him from the Cabinet, after he had won the seat with a good margin would have jolted him. He was frail and needed medical treatment. "I did not want him to feel dumped at a time he badly required emotional support," Shivraj had reasoned to me over the telephone. There are many such examples of his kind nature which many politicians and others have told me.

Politically speaking, I have not seen him unnecessarily attacking his opponents and creating unseemly debates. Wanting to remain in the limelight of publicity is not his way. He attacks his political opponents largely on the floor of the Assembly or during political rallies, that too under provocation, but does not go out of his way to hit out at all and sundry. "I seriously object to foreign media calling names to India's Prime Minister Dr Manmohan Singh," Shivraj Singh said while talking to the American media, soon after

54  *Shivraj Singh And Rise Of Madhya Pradesh*

the renowned *TIME* magazine termed Dr Singh as 'Under Achiever' on its cover page. Talking about the incident, he later told me, "We are all Indians and as different political parties, we may have our own differences, but when I was in America, it was my duty to defend my country's Prime Minister. I am not the one who would have made (political) capital out of the controversy triggered by the magazine." In fact, he eschews it, unlike his Cabinet colleagues such as Kailash Vijayvargiya who recently took a dig at Digvijay Singh during the inauguration of the first interlinking river project. Vijayvargiya said: "Digvijay Singh had said Narmada-Kshipra river link project was impossible but it's a success. I now feel he may have cheated in his engineering exams (*India Today*, 24 February 2012). Vijayvargiya knows how to hog the limelight—good or bad. But Shivraj is different; he stays away from such remarks unless really required.

Yes, the river linking project was an incredible idea. Shivraj Singh told me in his state aircraft when flying from Delhi to Indore after his meeting with the PM and the FM for the gram support price request.

The gram support price issue later snowballed into a major conflict between Madhya Pradesh and the Centre. On 6 March 2014, the entire Shivraj Cabinet sat on a peaceful *dharna* in Bhopal and the whole state observed total *bandh* to protest what was called grave injustice with MP's farmers who lost more than ₹ 10,000 crore worth of crops in hailstorm and unseasonal rains (attributed to El Nino factor). In MP where the farm sector recorded unprecedented growth, farmers were subjected to huge damages due to the vagaries of nature. Shivraj went out of his way to show the farmers that his government stood with them in times of crisis. He relaxed loan recoveries and asked the Revenue Department to immediately assess the loss and start making payments. He stated that all other works be stopped and ₹ 2,000 crore be diverted from different ongoing works to help farmers.

About the river link project he said: "All my officers, irrigation and water resources department engineers and politicians were thinking it was an impossible project. I tried twice and gave up but again called a meeting much before the 2013 elections to explore the possibility and I am happy to say the Narmada Valley Development Authority (NVDA) officers did an excellent job...now Malwa region where the water table had gone down very deep, will be benefitted and dry Kshipra river will be full of water before the Simastha-2016."

Rajnish Vaish, IAS, vice-chairman of Narmada Valley Development Authority (NVDA) of MP Government says that the task of linking two rivers in a difficult terrain, requiring central forest clearance, survey of the whole area, construction of a stop dam, assessing the existing dams' strength and capacity, digging up the intake channel, lifting water through pipelines up to 406 m with limited time on hand, was no less than an engineering miracle. "We did it just in 12 months after the Chief Minister gave us a challenge in August 2012. The work began on this first of its kind project in India, in February 2013 and on 6 February 2014, Narmada waters started gushing out into the dry Kshipra river. It was indeed an exhilarating experience when around 9 pm that day we saw waters reaching Ujjaini village of Indore district," a visibly elated Vaish said. From Omkareshwar Dam near Badwah in Khandwa district to Sesaliya tank (58 mts lift) in Khargone district and from Sesaliya to Simrol in Indore district, a further lifting of 348 meters—in all 406 meters water lifting was a stupendous task by any standards. The engineering marvel was that the Narmada water pumping speed was 5000 litres per second through the 47 km long pipeline to the dry bed of Kshipra.

## 56 *Shivraj Singh And Rise Of Madhya Pradesh*

The NS Link (Kshipra is also spelt as Shipra) was first thought of some time in early 1990s. In 1998, ₹ 38 crore was sanctioned by the then Congress Government to make a DPR ( detailed project report) of the same but then again the engineers and other bureaucrats termed it as non-feasible. NGOs like SANDRP of Himanshu Thakkar and Shripad Dharmadhikary and Rehmat from 'Manthan' opposed it on environmental grounds and raised many other issues protesting the project.

Till 2004, no one talked about it. Shivraj, getting reports of spreading desert from adjoining Rajasthan into MP's districts of Rajgarh, Shajapur, Ujjain and parts of Dhar and Indore where the ground water level was depleting fast and affecting vegetation tracts, decided once again to revive it but gave up in the face of opposition by officials. Finally, he with Chief Secretary R Parshuram, during a review meeting of the NVDA on 8 August 2012, asked Vaish, a low-profile, honest officer, if he could pick up the gauntlet. Vaish agreed and the Chief Secretary immediately sanctioned ₹ 432 crore to take Narmada into Kshipra—both ancient rivers—with just 14 months in hand. Shivraj's perseverance and ability to visualise something like this is quite commendable.

The NVDA team of technocrats, led by engineer-turned-IAS officer, Vaish, worked day and night and completed the Herculean task on a PPP model, while still saving Government money to the tune of ₹ 36 crore. With any such ambitious scheme, close to the heart of the CM, additional funds would have been sanctioned without many questions asked. But that was the hallmark of this innovative project (once dumped by the Congress Government as being almost impossible).

Besides providing water for the religious event in Ujjain in 2016, the NS Link Project has emerged as a life-saver for many districts of Malwa region. The *sangam* (confluence) spot of the two rivers at Ujjani has overnight become a new tourism centre where close to 25,000 people took a holy dip on 'Maha Shivratri' (a big festival of the devotees of Lord Shiva, on 27 February, 2014), celebrating the arrival of the Narmada, one of the sacred rivers in India. Vaish said, "It would bring prosperity to Malwa farmers with water availability in rivers and ensure the recharging of ground water over the next few years without any environmental loss." The forest clearance was obtained in a record 51 days from Delhi.

Shivraj Singh took all his cabinet colleagues to Ujjaini on 18 February, 2014 to hold an official meeting on the banks of the confluence.

On 26 January, at Vidisha when he unfurled the Republic Day flag he said, *"Aao banaye apna Madhya Pradesh."* He called upon a joint action of citizens and the Government to make MP the top ranking State in the country.

Shivraj, having accomplished the truly challenging task of linking the two rivers, had gone to meet an ailing Vajpayee in Delhi to seek his blessings in early 2014. As is public knowledge, Vajpayee is not physically in a position to recognise people, yet Shivraj made the attempt to apprise Vajpayee of his pet project.

❧❧❧❧

# Chapter - 5

# GOVERNANCE

If Shivraj Singh led his party to a record third time victory, it became possible, as various media reports also said, due to his good governance, among other factors. He himself says: "BJP is committed to *sushasan* (good governance)." Governance patterns at different times have depended largely on the party's own ideologies, as also the ruling leaders' personal understanding of the problems faced by people from time to time. Governance also includes delivery mechanisms and adherence to rules and regulations that are in vogue at any given time. There have been provincial governments in India which amended the obsolete or cumbersome rules that impeded the growth of a state.

Among many truly unique measures in governance and policy interventions that Madhya Pradesh witnessed, conducting 'panchayats' for various castes, women and youths, perhaps tops the list of Shivraj Singh Government's art of governance. I also call it his 'social engineering in a very intelligent and emotional manner'. These 'panchayats' are not the three-tier panchayats which are covered by the MP Panchayati Raj Act of 1993 (amended from time to time). The story and thought behind these panchayats is indeed interesting.

Any government belonging to any party in India—be it in Delhi or in a provincial capital—has had umpteen number of policies framed to benefit people since India's Independence. Some of them did actually benefit people. For instance, the land reforms of West Bengal that enabled Communist leader Jyoti Basu win elections for many years or the overall infrastructure development or the telecom revolution brought in by Rajiv Gandhi or corruption-free administration that Narendra Modi has provided to Gujaratis over the past 10 years or the road network provided by the Union Government and so on.

There are many many more, known and unknown, centrally-aided or exclusively Government of India schemes implemented across the country in free India over the past seven decades.

But in many cases, policies that were framed by civil servants having little direct connect with people, failed or succeeded partially. Faulty implementation and unchecked corruption were the main causes of failures, as we all know. Rajiv Gandhi went on record as the new PM of this country stating in Mumbai in 1985, that only 15 paise of a rupee that is sanctioned in Delhi reached the ultimate beneficiary for whom the rupee was sanctioned. No prizes for guessing how much of that 15 paise actually percolates down to the last man today when corruption has grown manifold under different political parties in various states...not to speak of an economist-driven Central Government of the UPA-II. Incidentally, the government in Delhi is remote-controlled by late Rajiv Gandhi's widow, Sonia and his son, Rahul (both have no official position in the government, per se) and has come to be known as the most corrupt government ever! The 2-G scam, the Commonwealth Games scam, subsidies scam are too oft-repeated to require fresh mention here.

Governance    61

If official policies were translating into benefits, millions of people living in the 651 districts (year 2012)—both, the approachable as well as the remote districts of this vast country—would never have faced problems like malnutrition deaths, hunger, poverty, housing issues, illiteracy, women's safety and dignity, absence of electricity, roads and water and so on. The Planning Commission too did not have to define 'poverty' in rural India and in urban India after 65 years of India's Independence. But that's a different story altogether!

## Holding Unique Panchayats

In Madhya Pradesh, the 'panchayats' organised by Shivraj were different in nature, concept and approach, than most other schemes or policies of any government. First, it was unique that as many as 37 such panchayats were held and most of them were held at the Chief Minister's official residence. Secondly, decisions taken on the spot were immediately notified, budgetary sanctions from the finance department obtained and required action taken by concerned departments. Most importantly, there was a personal touch provided by the CM who would remain present throughout and give on-the-spot solutions wherever it was feasible. The myriad participants used to have lunch with the Chief Minister on the sprawling lawns of his residence, and their transportation, board-lodging were arranged by the government free of cost.

The first such panchayat was held for women on 30 July 2006, within eight months of Shivraj Singh taking office as a greenhorn Chief Minister. He had neither been a minister nor a *sarpanch* nor a mayor. His understanding and experience of running an administration in a large state like MP was thus zero. Extremely low on confidence while dealing with highly-educated IAS officials, he however knew one thing much better than the members of the elite service: the pains of poor people. Girija Shankar, a veteran journalist and political analyst, says that Shivraj always scores over many of his peers due to his personality. "He comes from a very small village and shares the villagers' and poor people's problems like his own. He looks for solutions," he says adding, "if the Dalit agenda of Digvijay Singh government had been conceived and implemented by Shivraj Singh, perhaps it would not have been the fiasco which it turned out to be."

After the stupendous success of the women's panchayats, similar ones followed for the distressed farmers, tribals, forest workers, village *kotwars* (night watchmen), scheduled castes, small-scale entrepreneurs, different artisans, farm labourers, disabled persons, general category poor communities, construction workers, fishermen, self-help groups (SHGs), rickshaw pullers, *mandi hammal* (coolies in market places), urban domestic maid servants, street vendors, senior citizens, advocates, students, Panchayati Raj representatives, youths, barbers, leather artisans, bamboo craftsmen and the nomadic and semi-nomadic castes.

The first one organised after his victory in December 2013 was on 16 February 2014—for drivers and conductors of the unorganized sector, rickshaw drivers and truckers.

The CM not only listened to the drivers and conductors— over 3,500—for over three hours, he announced setting up of a ₹ 10 crore corpus fund for those who may meet with an eventuality like an accident. Since I have had the occasion to attend a couple of these, if not all, I know it is not a political leader's populist measure or a lip service that the CM tries to provide. These panchayats are an exception: they have left a lasting impact across communities and sectors. For instance, after announcing the ₹ 10 crore fund for them,

Shivraj Singh appealed to them to give up drinking while driving their vehicles. *"Sare log aaj haath uthao aur kasam khao ki daru peekar gadi nahi chalaoge aur ho sake to daru peena band karoge aaj se hi* (Raise your hands and take a vow to give up liquor while driving and if possible for life)." Over 7,000 hands went up in response to the CM's emotional appeal that touched their hearts.

Chhindwara Chalak Sangh's Jaswant Singh demanded a compulsory insurance scheme while Ajay Tripathi of Rewa suggested working hours limitation and compulsory rest for drivers, at which Shivraj narrated his own agony. "In 1998, I was on my campaign trail late in the night; the whole day my driver was doing duty and late night when we were returning home to Vidisha, I met with a severe accident and was hospitalized for many days… it was not the driver's fault but mine as he was tired and sleepy and I was still asking him to drive me home… as a result we collided with a tree in the dead of night… that day I decided to take care of all my drivers."

As he narrated his own story everyone listened to it in rapt attention as it touched their hearts. A CM talking of their welfare when no one had even asked them for a glass of water was a rare experience for all of them. They had seen the CM house for the first time and interacting with the CM on a one-to-one basis was like a dream. Shivraj told them, "I want you and your family to be happy. Since you are the backbone of our economy, it's my duty to look after your needs." Then he made a few announcements, including supply of ₹ 1 per kg rice to them just like the BPL card holders. He also announced the making of their I-cards for the various government schemes and listened to their many suggestions patiently.

Transport Commissioner Sanjay Chaudhary, IPS, Principal Secretary (Transport) Pramod Agarwal, IAS, CM's Principal Secretaries Manoj Shrivastava, IAS, and SK Mishra, IAS and

Transport Minister Bhupendra Singh were all there overseeing the arrangements and helping to solve their problems on the spot. "My idea of panchayats is two-pronged: first, listen to their problems in their own words and secondly, provide schemes so their incomes are enhanced," Shivraj explained to me after the panchayat. He said, "It is not only that we organise the panchayats and earn on the spot praise for the tall promises made. I personally follow up with each department on a regular basis to take things to a logical conclusion. Financial outlays are already earmarked so the file is not stopped by the finance department."

For the last seven years, periodic panchayats have been held, taking the number to 37 and making hundreds of families happy and content.

Having seen Madhya Pradesh inside out for years, I see in these events more than a mere congregation of people to be made happy with the CM's presence and some psychological spin. A brilliant thought executed intelligently, much better than Digvijay Singh's surprise village contact programmes which, for various reasons, did not help him beyond a point.

In other words, from July 2006 until September 2013, this exercise continued with periodic intervals and decisions were taken after listening to the problems of people from different communities and vocations. Such decisions were not just decisions but were converted into state policies as and when required.

Decisions like the hike in student stipends for tribal areas; for farmers, abolition of the cess on farm implements; creation of women help desks in urban police stations; 50% reservation in local bodies for women were announced on the spot. Store purchase rules for small entrepreneurs were amended; pension schemes for construction labourers were declared; *tendu patta* collection rates were raised; state fish policy for fishermen was announced; a youth commission was set up for students. The Chief Minister's Pilgrimage Scheme (Mukhyamantri Teerth Darshan Yojana) was the outcome of a meeting of the CM with senior citizens at a panchayat meant for the elders. Many more such decisions were taken but the basis of these panchayats was Shivraj Singh's interaction with cross-sections of people and the first-hand feedback he received from them. Being a very accessible politician whose heart really bleeds for the poor and the backward, he can sense where the shoe is pinching. "If policies are made in air-conditioned rooms of the *sachivalaya* (secretariat) by secretaries who do not meet people and have no ear to the ground, they are bound to fail," the CM reasoned.

The governance pattern in the country has generally been that policies are either made in secretariats and ministries and announced on the floor of Parliament or State Assembly or during political meetings as merely political announcements by a chief minister or a departmental minister.

Digvijay Singh, during his tenure as the Congress CM for 10 years, had started a Gram Sampark Abhiyan—village contact programme. It was once a year, for a week. Those days it was considered unique as the CM himself would swoop down in a state chopper in any of the small hamlets of the undivided Madhya Pradesh unannounced. It gave sleepless nights to the district administration but people appeared happy. Digvijay's idea was to listen to the villagers' problems and also check with them if the benefits of his government's policies were reaching them. The spot check operation of Diggi Raja, as he was fondly called, did make headlines all over the country. "At 55, he has won the 'Model CM' tag solely on the strength of the elementary tools of governance and development," wrote Ajit K Jha, Associate Editor of *Sunday Express*. AK Bhattacyarya, Resident Editor *Business Standard*, had this to say:

"Whatever the pros and cons of the flying visits, there is no doubt Digvijay Singh gets an unvarnished, first-hand account of how the people feel." A freelance journalist Harihar Swarup wrote sometime in the year 2000, "Digvijay Singh is creating a revolution in the rural areas of his sprawling state."

Many more journalists had travelled with the CM to see first-hand what he was doing. Chief secretaries of the time such as KS Sharma and AV Singh used to accompany him on some of his tours or his bright, honest secretary R Gopalkrishnan, who passed away just a couple of years ago. Unfortunately for Digvijay Singh, three years after the state was divided into two, the Congress Party was thrown out of power and is yet to come back. The reasons for the Congress defeat were many but absence of good governance was the major one.

Shivraj's panchayats are more participatory. The people were asked their problems and during the day-long sittings the concerned department's ministers and officers were present and decisions were taken then and there in most cases. This enhanced the faith of people in the government in general and Shivraj Singh in particular. No wonder then, he first won in 2008 and then bettered his performance in 2013.

This is not to indicate that these panchayats were the single most important reason for the BJP's victories in 2008 and 2013 but yes, they did have their positive impact across communities and various professions. There had been similar schemes or policies to redress people's problems implemented by earlier governments but somehow they could not translate into votes nor did they benefit people a great deal.

The major difference between the mass village contact programme of Digvijay and panchayats of Shivraj is that during

Digvijay's rule, the follow-up of people's problems was very poor, but come 2006, the difference was there for everyone to see. The difference lay in the sincere approach or lack of it.

## Mukhyamantri Teerth Darshan Yojana

The Mukhyamantri Teerth Darshan Yojana was a scheme in which few people benefitted but it had tremendous psychological impact on elders who were taken to a religious shrine of their choice on a state-sponsored pilgrimage.

Energy Minister, Rajendra Shukla from Rewa says that during one of the recent campaigns an old and illiterate lady straightaway told the CM that if he took her on a *teerth*, she would vote for him. The CM smiled in agreement but also realised how popular the small scheme had become in remote, backward areas of his state.

Shukla says that Shivraj's mingling with rural and poor people with ease gives him an advantage over many others. He keeps travelling all over the state and keeps talking of development and development alone. "Because of his approach we see a change in the work culture across MP." Shukla says that when the CM decided that 24 hour power was to be provided, the entire department from top to bottom started talking the same language.

Among the governance and unique schemes under Shivraj Singh, I have considered only four important ones that helped better governance and made people happy and empowered in some way or the other:

- Panchayats
- Teerth Darshan Yojana
- The massive work of making agriculture a profitable business.
- Welfare of women and girl child.

There are many others like industries promotion, maintenance

## 68 *Shivraj Singh And Rise Of Madhya Pradesh*

of law and order, building roads and guaranteeing education which were also implemented.

All these helped Shivraj come back to power again.

On the face of it, the Mukhayamantri Teerth Darshan Yojana was among the smallest schemes of the BJP government but its impact was far reaching and very satisfying for Shivraj who thought of it and quickly got it implemented.

The scheme was conceived for those helpless senior citizens who either have no money or no family support to go on religious tours. A scheme was devised by which they were offered hassle-free travel to a religious destination of their choice. They were taken by special trains from Bhopal or Rewa, Indore or Ujjain or Jabalpur to the country's famous shrines—Rameswaram, Kanyakumari, Nanded, Badrinath, Kedarnath (Uttarakhand), Kashi (UP), Tirupati (AP) Shravan Belgola (Karnataka), Velankanni church in Tamil Nadu, Shirdi in Maharashtra, Gaya (Bihar) Ajmer Sharif (Rajasathan), Vaishno Devi (J&K) and so on.

Any discerning reader would realise that Hindus, Sikhs, Muslims and Christians have all been included in this scheme with no discrimination whatsoever. The CM's Principal Secretary Manoj Shrivastava, a senior IAS officer who first introduced the precis to the Cabinet for Teerth Darshan Yojana, told this author: "Ours is a comprehensive, all-inclusive approach that leads to the overall development of the state. All Madhya Pradeshis are the same for us."

The much-hyped scheme was launched on 3 September 2012 by LK Advani (by flagging off a train from Bhopal to Rameswaram) along with the CM, underscoring the importance the MP Government was attaching to its unique scheme which had more of an emotional touch than an official one.

The MP Government tied up with the Indian Railways and paid directly to the Railways for the tickets and food. One attendant per bogey from the railways and one from the MP Government was deputed, besides local conveyance and stay etc was pre-planned and trips made comfortable as far as possible. Those above 65 years were entitled to take an attendant with them.

An officer connected with the scheme in the Revenue Department said that the file regarding this particular scheme took seven to eight months in the state's secretariat to ensure proper and hassle-free implementation almost seamlessly to the last point. So far more than 800 trains have left MP for different locations carrying thousands of people to their Gods and what have they brought back? A satisfied family of elders blessing Shivraj from the bottom of their hearts.

"I never thought of any political mileage from this kind of a plan," Shivraj said while talking to me one day just before the elections. "It gave me huge internal satisfaction, as being a Chief Minister I could fulfill desires of those who could never ever think of going to faraway places."

In modern days when family bonds are not as strong as they were earlier, this has come as a boon for senior citizens.

Clearly, over 1.5 lakh people have emerged as the new committed brand ambassadors of Madhya Pradesh. They have made Shivraj Singh popular through word of mouth in all corners of the country as a Chief Minister with a heart and soul.

ର୍ତ୍ତ୍ତ୍ତ

Chapter - 6

# AGRARIAN MIRACLE

At a time when the changing profile of a typical Indian village was posing problems for the Indian rulers and planners on several fronts—growing poverty, rural influx into urban centres, resultant pressures on urban infrastructure and collapse of rural economy with cities being touted as growth engines in the globalised economic scenario—Madhya Pradesh tried to swim against the tide.

One of the dramatic differences the Shivraj Government brought about in a 'developing state' was turning agriculture into a profitable and sustainable business when elsewhere in India, it was forcing farmers to commit suicides or live in abject poverty. Globally too, farm-related figures were not very encouraging from '70s onwards. In 1979, 18% of the official development aid worldwide was directed at agriculture; by 2004, that amount sank to 3.5%. "Agriculture lost its glitter," the world-famous weekly *Time* (26 October 2009) declared, quoting UNO's Food and Agriculture Organisation (FAO). It said, "years of neglect took their toll on the world's farmers, laying the groundwork for a crisis. In India, the agricultural produce which was between 4% and 6% during the Green Revolution (1960s), dropped to 2% or so after the '80s."

MP was no exception. No one could read the writing on the wall

## 72 *Shivraj Singh And Rise Of Madhya Pradesh*

despite the deepening food crisis all over the world. "At a meeting of authors and editors of the International Assessment of Agriculture Knowledge, Science and Technology for Development (IAASTD) in South Africa, in June 2007, the theme of crisis in agriculture was put forward as a possible framing for what would become the Assessment's Synthesis Report. However, this idea was rejected because it was thought to exaggerate the prevailing conditions. When the report was launched in April 2008, food riots in Haiti and elsewhere revealed the severity of the agriculture situation. The food crisis was followed by unprecedented increases in energy prices that helped to define how people were beginning to think about the relation between poverty, energy, land and natural resource use," said a research paper (A messy confrontation of a crisis in agricultural science) in the *Economic and Political Weekly*, dated 16 January 2010.

It was about the time when an agriculture revolution was taking its baby steps in Madhya Pradesh. It would be tantamount to lying to say that Shivraj Singh knew of the global agriculture scenario and scientific debates at the highest levels of international policy framing bodies in 2007 but his rural background and restlessness to do something for farmers had already translated into an agro-vision for the state. The results came later.

The last five years or more have seen the changed conditions of life and work of thousands of farmers across the State. This has naturally affected their attitude towards the government and their voting patterns. Among the main reasons that brought Singh back into power in 2013 was his sustained effort for the overall agricultural reform process that bore fruits by the time the BJP went into poll mode. This was an example of good governance, ie understanding the needs of the people and then framing policies accordingly to deliver results, rather than delivering empty promises—an art our

Shivraj Singh addressing a gathering in Vidisha during an election campaign. Also seen are Uma Bharti, M M Joshi and Raghavji Bhai (top); Shivraj during his college days (centre left); At the culmination of BJYM Mashal Yatra in Bhopal in 1988 (Centre right); With former Prime Minster Atal Behari Vajpayee and MP Narendra Singh Tomar (bottom left)
Courtesy: Sanjeev Gupta, Shiv Chaube.

Shivraj with wife Sadhana during their wedding on 8 May 1992 (Top left); Shivraj has always been a favourite with the elderly. (Top right); Shivraj bows before little girls at a function in Vidisha with wife Sadhana helping him. (Bottom right); Shivraj, the encouraging 'Mama' for girls in Madhya Pradesh (Bottom left).
Courtesy: Vivek Pateria/Outlook; GPBRA; Bhalu Mondhe.

hivraj plays a *dholak* at a tribal gathering Top); Shivraj rides a bicycle as part of the reen Planet Bicycle Riders Association ampaign to save petrol, in 2008 (Bottom eft); Narendra Modi escorting Shivraj o the oath podium after BJP's record ictory in December 2013 (Bottom right). ourtesy : GPBRA; Madhyam; Anil Dixit/Dainik Bhaskar.

During women's panchayat in 2006 at CM house Bhopal (Top); Celebrarting Christmas on 25 December 2012 at CM house. Courtesy: Madhyam (Bottom)

At Shivraj Singh's residence in Bhopal after the BJP's thumping victory in the State Assembly elections in 2013 (Top); Sports buff Shivraj watching finals of Junior National Kho Kho Championship at Happy Wanderers Sports Ground in Indore (Centre left); With actor Raza Murad at an Eid function (Bottom).
Courtesy: BJP State Unit, Bhopal; Bhalu Mondhe; The Hindu Business Line.

Shivraj meeting the Japanese delegation at the CM office. (Top); Shivraj with South Africa's Free State leader Ace Magashule (Centre right); With investors in South Africa in August 2014. Also seen is Industries Minister of MP Yashodhara Raje. (Centre left); Shivraj Singh on the occasion of his three-day visit to Dubai when an MoU was signed between the Emirates official and Md Suleman Principal Secretary Industries (Bottom).

Receiving Krishi Karman Award for the first time in 2012 at the hands of President Pranab Mukherjee in New Delhi. Also seen is Union Agriculture Minister Sharad Pawar. Madhya Pradesh won the top agriculture state award for two years consecutively —2012 and 2013.

Shivraj Singh inspecting damaged crops at a farm in a village in Sehore district (Top); Shivraj having a direct interaction with the bureaucrats (Centre); During a visit to Dubai, Shivraj meets Diamond merchants. Industries Minister Yashodhra Raje Scindia also present (Bottom).
Courtesy MP Madhyam

politicians have mastered.

The agriculture revolution is largely responsible for removing the decades-old BIMARU tag from the state.

Despite being an agrarian country with close to 70% of the 120 crore odd Indian population depending directly or indirectly on agriculture, the sector remained neglected since Independence. The average growth in the sector was less than 2% at the national level which grew slightly towards the end of the twentieth century. All available statistics prove that sustainable agriculture was never a priority of the governments of the day nor were the poverty alleviation programmes linked to agricultural growth. So agriculture remained a low priority area, rural development did not take place and poverty kept mounting. After a decade of the Green Revolution of 1960s, Prime Minister Indira Gandhi had to give a clarion call of *garibi hatao* (eradicate poverty) in early 1970s and on the eve of the 2014 General Elections, the Congress is still talking of the same *garibi hatao*!

The vagaries of climate (unpredictable monsoon), anomalies in pricing structure, poor irrigation facilities, faulty credit facility framework, changes in government policies from time to time, Centre-state relations, support price imbroglio, lack of technological intervention and useful research, besides the absence of long-term policies, ensured that most of the small farmers remained in eternal debt and distress. Successive governments in Delhi and in states did little to contain the widespread agrarian failure.

## UPA's Promise

Though the National Common Minimum Programme of the UPA government had declared that it would arrest the decline in agriculture and provide substantial hike in the spending in rural areas to help cultivation, much of it remained on paper. Experts in the field say that the UPA tried to undo what NDA had done to reform the sector. "With the UPA government coming to power in 2004, the reforms process saw a considerable slowdown. Much of what was done by the NDA, and even earlier, was wholly or partly reversed during this regime, though in a piecemeal manner," writes Surinder Sud in his absorbing book, *The Changing Profile of Indian Agriculture.*

No wonder then that hundreds and thousands of sugarcane producers had descended upon Delhi on 19 November 2009 to protest against the government. Delhi witnessed massive traffic jams that day due to the mammoth rally. But that's not the issue; the issues were much larger and they had forced cane growers from the neighbouring states to come to Delhi and draw the government's attention to their multiple problems.

What UPA did for farmers in general, not only the cane growers, ahead of the Lok Sabha elections of 2009 was to waive country wide loans of farmers to the tune of a whopping ₹ 70,000 crore rather than providing lasting solutions to their problems. It was a populist measure of the UPA to garner votes on the eve of elections.

But the Manmohan Singh Government did not stop at that. Having accused its predecessor, the NDA, of ignoring the Indian farmers, it committed a blunder in allowing American multi-nationals to conduct their business in Indian agriculture sectors. In July 2005, Dr Manmohan Singh and President George Bush signed a treaty under the Indo-American Knowledge Initiative on Agriculture that gave free entry to large food corporations into India and use of dangerous fertilisers and pesticides at will, without assessing long-term damage to the soil.

*Agrarian Miracle* 75

Interestingly enough, it was an American researcher of repute (with work experience of over 50 years in India), Ms Joan P Mencher, who had blasted the move. In an interview to *Frontline* on 1 January 2010, she said: "People both in the West and in rural India are being manipulated to accept corporate approaches." She also opined that Indian [agricultural] scientists should focus on sustainable agriculture with emphasis on reforms from below... the food deficit was being used as a rationale to deprive farmers of their autonomy and traditional knowledge.

Who else should have known the importance of traditional knowledge better than the people of Madhya Pradesh? For it was in that a lasting experiment in nature-based agricultural practice was started in 1920s by a Briton. Sir Albert Howard, founder of Indian Science Congress, came to India as an imperial economic botanist to train Indian peasants in the art and science of chemical agriculture. Curiously enough, he ended up learning organic farming from the peasants instead and started treating them with respect as his teachers.

He came to Indore, now the commercial capital of MP, and once ruled by the Holkar princely dynasty sometime in 1923-24. Sir Howard devised a process for the manufacture of humus from vegetable and animal waste at the Institute of Plant Industry, Indore. He writes in his epochal book, *An Agricultural Testament* (first published in London in 1940): 'The Indore process was named after the Indian state in which it originated, in grateful remembrance of all that the Indore Darbar (Holkars) did to make my task in central India easier and more pleasant'.

His experiments for improving the agricultural produce were based on the foundation of organic use of fertilizers and improving soil fertility constantly. He did his research between 1924 and 1931 at Indore on the 300 acres of land leased by the Holkar Princely State for 99 years, to set up the Institute of Plant Industry that he founded in 1924. There was no scientific research facility in several of the central Indian states and thus the centre came to Indore, thanks to the foresight of Holkar Maharaj (Tukojirao). The Indore method for maintaining soil fertility by the manufacture of humus from vegetables and animal wastes was described by Sir Howard in an earlier book—*The Waste Products of Agriculture*, published in 1931. Howard says that the 'Indore Process' became so popular that many other countries adopted it over the years.

Yet, in most of the Indian states including Madhya Pradesh from where this unique agriculture research went out to the world, Indian agriculture got nothing more than lip service and farmers continued to lead lives in misery. This continued well after the country got its independence from the British. Paradoxically, it was the intelligent British scientist who gave the gift of 'Indore Process' to the world but we as a nation languished for decades together.

If we talk of the recent past, governments have not done much for the farming community. The turn of the century saw unprecedented suicides in many states, with Maharashtra leading the pack. Worst-affected states were Andhra Pradesh, Maharashtra, Karnataka and Kerala. Even in the present scenario, no great hope is held out for them. The once leading agro-state like Maharashtra, where cooperative movement had taken roots quite early and modern farming techniques were in vogue, saw things deteriorating over the years rather than improving, despite changes in technology and demand in foodgrains.

Maharashtra, for the first time in its history, took the largest ever loan of ₹ 2,000 crore to inject life into the problem-ridden sector. The loan was secured from the World Bank (₹ 650 crore), ADB (₹ 750 crore) and ₹ 600 crore from the International Fund for Agro Development (IFAD). The decision to make such big investments came after three-four years of the first farmer's suicide in the Vidarbha region of Maharashtra where a large number of farmers were driven to take the extreme step of ending their lives due to heavy debts. Maharashtra's agriculture went through a troubled phase at a time when the country's Agriculture and Food Minister, Sharad Pawar hailed from that state. Well-known for his dynamism and understanding of the sector Pawar, however, could do little to improve it despite his 10-year long stint in the same ministry. In a survey by *India Today* in 2001, Maharashtra's ranking in agriculture stood at 11th, with Punjab, Haryana and Tamil Nadu topping the list in that order. In 2013, it slid down a notch to 12th in the country. Agreed that agriculture is a state subject but Central policies and budgetary allocations do play an important role.

## The Visible Change

Unlike Maharashtra or Punjab, Madhya Pradesh was almost nowhere on the agricultural map of India for many decades after its birth in 1956, notwithstanding the unparalleled research at Indore that showed the right direction to farmers.

In the survey of states mentioned above, MP stood at 13th in 2005 and in 2009. But the situation changed thereafter as the efforts of the MP government started yielding fruits.

The year 2012 was a historic year, when MP was judged India's top state by the Government of India and was given the 'Krishi Karman Award' at the hands of the President of India. The same happened in 2013 when Shivraj Singh Chouhan received the award (of the earlier year) on 10 February 2014 from President Pranab

Mukherjee in Delhi, for the second year in a row. The award is given by the Ministry of Agriculture. The agriculture reforms of Madhya Pradesh that slowly began taking shape in 2006-07 took time to take roots but total focus and constant policy interventions in the field brought MP to the top and made farmers happy. Farming became a *labh ka dhandha* (profitable business) after all.

It is for this reason I have included in this book, the unprecedented agricultural growth due to the various successful schemes or projects of the government to show how good governance wins votes and also makes the state a welfare state. MP is now a talked-about State all over the country for its superb performance in many sectors and for fighting the economic slowdown in its own way.

How was the sector turned around? Was it easy to make agriculture a profitable business when urbanisation was growing at a very rapid speed and decadal growth was placed somewhere between 25% and 30%?

Surely not! It was indeed a huge and multi-disciplinary task that Shivraj Singh undertook. He reformed the sector while simultaneously infusing life into rural development as well. It was almost like turning the clock back!

As has been mentioned earlier, Shivraj is the son of a farmer from a small village. He had seen and suffered the travails of the marginal farmers and the farm labourers and therefore an overarching policy framework could be created in MP under his dynamic leadership.

Soon after taking over the chief ministership, he had declared that *kheti ko labh ka dhanda banana mera sapna hai* (making agriculture a profitable business is my dream). Unlike other politicians, he did not just announce his intentions to the people of MP and left it at that. He rigourously followed them up with a series of steps—financial support and framing policies with all sincerity, year after year.

## From Files To Fields

It all began with a *kisan* panchayat on 30 August 2006—less than 10 months after Shivraj took over the office of the CM. It was Balram Jayanti when the second of the unique 'panchayats' (a big participatory meeting of stakeholders and beneficiaries of a sector) took place at the CM house, the first being for women on July 30 at the same venue. Organising it on Balram Jayanti was again aimed at integrating socio-cultural calender with the rigors of modern governance.

Sops for the peasant community rained like never before. As many as 40 pro-farmers decisions were taken on one single day in the presence of hundreds of farmers from all over the state. Then gradually, the CM's announcements were taken out of the official files to the fields.

A senior bureaucrat shared an interesting incident: the CM and a few officers were returning from the India Today Conclave in 2007. In the state aircraft they were discussing farmers and the issue of short-term crop loans interest. Shivraj was all for bringing the rate down drastically in one shot but one of his IAS officer secretaries suggested that such a populist measure would put cooperative banks in severe trouble and their existing structure would be disturbed. But the CM remained steadfast. He brought it down from 16% to 9% and, over the next few years it was lowered to 1%.

The whopping 16% rate was enough to break the back of any farmer. By 2012, the rate came down to zero, making MP the first such state in the country to be able to do so. In the year 2013, ₹ 11,209 crore was distributed as crop loans. The growth in crop loans for the last three years in MP has reached 89%. The resolve of a politician can work wonders if he sincerely wants to do something concrete for the people. What better example would anyone need than this?

*80   Shivraj Singh And Rise Of Madhya Pradesh*

On a Sunday afternoon, on the eve of his visit to Delhi for receiving the second national agro-award, Shivraj told me at his residence: "We decided to make agriculture a profitable activity and to help realise the dream we took a series of bold decisions that have proved beneficial for the welfare of the farmers' community... 0% interest rate and setting up a Krishi Cabinet (Agriculture Cabinet) were two of the many important decisions that transformed the sector in the state."

Traditionally, the agriculture growth rate in MP had been 3-4% which grew to a double digit figure in 2012-13 and 2013-14, pushing it to the top of the table, across the country.

Agriculture Production Commissioner (APC) MM Upadhyay, IAS, tells me that it was not that they took decisions on a piecemeal basis. "There was a grand vision of the CM which was converted into an overarching policy of the state. Many departments other than agriculture also made their own working plans to gel with the policy of making agriculture a profitable business and results started pouring in only after the combined effort." Starting bonus payments to the farmers, in addition to the minimum support price (MSP) to wheat which was later extended to rice and maize, strengthened the farmers economically.

Cooperatives, water resources, energy, finance, revenue, rural development, animal husbandry and such allied departments were made to achieve one target: make farmers happy; make their business profitable. They all worked in the same direction; regular reviews of targets were done, various hurdles removed and encouraging results ensued automatically.

In a democracy, public servants are expected to deliver results, something Madhya Pradesh witnessed in the last few years with the political boss leaving no stone unturned to achieve overall growth.

Narayan Singh Balmukund Dangi, a marginal farmer from Purneiya village, about 22 km from the district headquarters of Vidisha, (a district known for its quality wheat) said he was not a BJP sympathiser but had not seen a government like this which did what it said. "Our family has been in the agriculture business for three generations but only in the past three-four years, we are able to make both ends meet... *ye to kamal hi ho gaya hai* (we are witnessing something remarkable), a jubilant Dangi said.

However, when he spoke with me, he said that while the government was helping a lot and agriculture officers in the fields were extending all help and doing everything possible for the cultivators, "*Ooperwala dekho kya nainsafi kar raha hai hamare saath* (why is God being so unfair to us), pointing to unseasonal rains that lashed many parts of the country, including MP, in the last week of February. According to a leading Hindi daily of Madhya Pradesh, *Dainik Bhaskar* (Bhopal, dated 27 February 2014) the torrential rain, accompanied by heavy hailstorm, was the first of its kind in the 88 years history of this month. Recorded rainfall of that day (26 February 2014) was 3.96 cm in eight hours.

Standing crops in Bhopal, Vidisha, Ashok Nagar, Rajgarh, Guna, Sehore districts were damaged beyond repair and the Revenue Department estimated more than 50% damage at a time when bumper crops were expected in the markets.

MP is the largest wheat-producing state. Around 30-35 varieties of wheat are extensively grown in MP's different agro-zones. Most popular and widely-grown variety is Lok-1 (around 50%) in the Malwa region. It has a good yield of 40-50 quintals per HA. Other popular varieties are: Purna (HI-1544) used for food, Navin Chandosi (HI-1418), HI-1531, HW-2004, HI-1500 and Sujata. These varieties contribute 25% of the total variety of wheat produced in this region.

Apart from these, other varieties which are popular and grown in the remaining 25% area are Duram, Poshan (HI-8663) and Malav Shakti (HI-8498). These are in high demand for export purposes and are also used for making Thuli, Dalia, etc says Sudhir Soni, a quality seed grower from Indore.

MP also produces soyabean, *chana, jowar* and paddy (rice) but in wheat it has broken all records for two successive years and Shivraj strongly feels that soon MP will beat Punjab. "So far we are the third largest wheat-producing state in the country and we contribute 17.5% of country's demand," informs the CM.

"The bottomline is that a BIMARU state produced 17.5% of the country's total wheat production in 2013 (161.25 lakh MT) which was 72.08 lakh MT in 2008. And of the total agricultural produce of the country, MP's contribution, in different foodgrain production, was as large as 11.2% (277.84 lakh MT)," said Upadhyay.

The farmers' easy access to credit is an important yardstick to gauge the growth in farming sector of any State. If loans availed by MP farmers were ₹ 3,300 crore in 2006, the figure zoomed to ₹ 11,209 crore in 2013-2014—a quantum jump of over 320%.

The state took important steps that directly benefited the farmers such as making them available quality seeds, technology, pesticides and fertilisers. The consistent supply of quality seeds made farmers happy. Seeds of wheat, soyabean, chana and pulses were grown and made available to the lakhs and lakhs of farmers. MP topped the list of seed supplier states with a record production of 43.95 lakh quintals, followed by AP (40.04), UP (37.08 lakh), Maharashtra (10.1 lakh) and Gujarat (5.5 lakh), in 2013.

Now MP has become one of the biggest producers of *chana* (gram), accounting for 30-35% of country's production. It has been sown over 35 lakh ha and the State expects production of 47 lakh MT in 2014 Rabi season, according to a report in *Hindustan Times*, Bhopal, 16 February 2014. But the Centre did not cooperate with MP on the Minimum Support Price (MSP) which led Shviraj Singh to Delhi to meet the Prime Minister and Finance Minister after his meeting with Agriculture Minister Sharad Pawar did not bring results. At a Cabinet meeting in Bhopal on 26 February, it was decided that the entire Cabinet would go and meet President Pranab Mukherjee on this vexed issue. As the gram purchase matter heated up on the eve of Lok Sabha elections, the purely farm issue acquired a political colour. The state required over ₹ 5,000 crore to procure so much gram across MP and expected the Central Government to chip in, which it refused. Sharad Pawar apparently expressed his inability and directed the CM to meet the Prime Minister and the Finance Minister. That amply showed the UPA coalition's internal strains.

In a recent in-depth article in *The Economic Times*, M Rajshekhar says, "Under Sharad Pawar's long tenure at Krishi Bhawan (Delhi), there is evidence that the larger farmer has benefited more than the smaller farmer, the trader more than the farmer, the powerful more than the powerless."

Well, if agriculture started looking up in MP, it was also due to the Energy Department's laying of separate feeder lines for agriculture. This provided uninterrupted power supply for a minimum guaranteed period of eight hours, though government also claimed that most of the villages in MP got 24 hour supply. Separate feeder lines were first installed in Gujarat but MP also worked on the scheme successfully, investing a huge amount of capital expenditure. Md Suleman, IAS, Principal Secretary of the Energy Department, says MP's separate agri-feeder is among the most widespread networks in the country, connecting 43,517 villages with an 11 KW line, comprising over 70,000 km. Over 700 transformers of 25

KW were set up to regulate the power supply. If the power situation was worse in 2003 at 4,834 MW, 10 years down the line it grew to 10,231 MW in 2013. Clearly, it was a 'gamechanger' on the eve of elections in MP which comprises a large number of villages. Rajendra Shukla, Energy Minister in conversation with me, said he saw a group of MP State Electricity Board (MPSEB) engineers almost dancing and greeting each other after a function of the *Atal Jyoti Abhiyan* which the chief minister inaugurated in Malwa region last year. The scheme focusses on providing uninterrupted power supply to urban as well as rural areas of Madhya Pradesh. Shukla said that when the entire department worked with a singleness of purpose to supply power 24 x 7 from top to bottom and with a changed and positive mindset, achieving the goal became much easier.

Shivraj Singh was of the view that: "The 24 hour power supply ensured total social-economic change in the state as industries, agriculture and domestic use in villages boosted overall development in the state."

Making agriculture a profitable business was of course not an easy task and much beyond the reach of the agriculture department alone. So when the Chief Minister realised that work was little tardy, a small working group of Cabinet Ministers was formed and given Cabinet's powers. It was called the 'Agriculture Cabinet' and it came into being in June 2011.

The BJP ruled Karnataka too had this kind of an arrangement but owing to various reasons it could not succeed there. R Parshuram, IAS, the then Development Commissioner of the state was given the charge of this Cabinet even as the incumbent Chief Secretary, Avni Vaish continued in his job. There were reports that suggested that the CM did not much appreciate Vaish's style of functioning and at one point of time had made up his mind to shift him and replace him with Parshuram. On his part, Vaish who had a long stint in the US as consultant with the World Bank in Washington, too, did not much alter his working to suit his boss, like his successor did. Shivraj did talk to some of his advisors on bureaucratic matters about this issue, but then shelved the plan and got his agriculture-related works done through Parshuram, who later became the Chief Secretary. He also got an extension of six months with a nod from Government of India, becoming the first such top bureaucrat in the state.

Shivraj Singh wrote a letter to the Prime Minister, Dr Manmohan Singh, pleading for Parshuram's extension and got it done. "I had many projects in the pipeline and to complete them I needed continuity at the apex of the administrative set up, especially when I was already busy with election work," the CM had reasoned to me.

Coming back to the complete metamorphosis of the farm sector and putting it on fast track of growth, the state ensured that first the interest on loans was slashed, then seeds and fertilizers were provided in abundance. These were followed by providing electricity. The almost non-existent commodity during the Congress regime became available in ample supply. But what was more important was irrigating the fields after one had power. The canals which had broken down due to disuse for years were repaired, their linings set right and incomplete irrigation projects were completed on war footing. As water started gushing into the fields, farmers' faces shone with hope. As per records, if in 2003, 7.05 lakh ha land was under cultivation, it rose to 25 lakh ha in 2013. "It has happened nowhere in the country that so much agri-land is under irrigation," Upadhyay said, adding, "this almost completed our job."

Amul Urdhwareshe, the executive vice-chairman of Sahyog Mircofinance Limited, working in several districts of the state says, "In Harda where we have set up milk collection centres to help small

86  *Shivraj Singh And Rise Of Madhya Pradesh*

farmers, besides other activities, the farmers have grown steadily."

"Harda is a rare district where 80% area is under cultivation and 70% is irrigated and in the neighbouring area of Badi Bareli in Raisen district, the Barna reservoir canal network has brought about crop pattern changes in its command area making farmers grow richer cash crops," Urdhwareshe says from his first-hand experience from the field. He says rural poverty will also vanish if proper agro-growth is maintained by the state government year-on-year, backed by research and putting in investment when required.

Hemant Soni, Chairman of the Akriti Group, echoes this sentiment on the basis of his cane-growing experience. His group has been benefited in Narsinghpur district where, thanks to the recent improvement in the irrigation facilities, sugarcane cultivation has steadily gone up paving the way for establishing sugar factories by his group and others. The mere providing of irrigation facilities had a superb chain effect: It brought investment, made farmers self-reliant, created jobs and generated wealth. MP was a little known state on the sugarcane map of India but it is rapidly it is picking up, mainly in the Narmada belt (Western Narmada Valley) from Jabalpur to Narsinghpur, Soni added. There are 19 sugar factories in MP, of which 15 are operating—three in cooperative sector and 12 in private sector—with sizeable crushing capacity. There is a possibility of cane growing catching up with favourable agro-climatic conditions. Soni says, "In Narsinghpur district cultivators have adopted intercropping of gram, wheat, onion, garlic and increased their profitability."

As per the APC, when the crop came into the market, the state was there again extending a helping hand to the farmer. The unique scheme of e-*uparjan* (electronic procurement) was brought into force by which hassle-free environment was provided to the farmer to sell his produce. "We used to inform 10 lakh farmers through one crore SMSs the dates of purchasing, the rates at the several primary cooperative purchase centres spread across rural MP and so on. MP established the first computerised and most elaborate procurement arrangement through primary societies," a beaming Upadhyay said, adding, "since the CM was attaching highest importance to agriculture, the bureaucracy had to give results."

Warehousing facilities also increased in MP with huge airtight silo bags made available for storage. A composite logistic hub at the cost of ₹ 140 under PPP (Public Private Partnership) mode is being built in Pawarkheda, Hoshangabad district. The storage facility, which was 79 lakh MT in 2010, grew to 115 lakh MT in 2013 and 152 lakh MT is projected in 2014, making MP the largest storage capacity state in the country with a 32% jump in four years. People in agri-business feel the State Government should, on priority basis, invite industrialists to use this bumper crop and set up food processing plants (for making dalia, thuli, breads and biscuits) for generating employment and collecting tax revenues.

A jubilant Shivraj Singh puts it like this: "My dream was to see a smiling farmer and social change through him and I am happy to have realised it during my tenure itself despite numerous hurdles that the government encountered at every step." He also wonders why previous CMs did not take much interest in this sector which feeds millions of people and keeps villages happy and the state growing.

ଓଓଓଓ

## Chapter - 7

# SOCIAL CONCERNS

Many years ago when he was a newly elected Member of Parliament, Shivraj Singh, moved by the deplorable condition of the poor people in villages, decided to organise mass marriages of girls whose parents could ill-afford spending even ₹ 5,000 on their daughter's wedding. He would collect the required money from friends and add some of his own resources for the noble cause. His wife Sadhana would also join him to bless the newly-weds.

"It was like a personal mission for me as I always knew how difficult it was for a father to marry off a daughter and this was among the chief reasons people did not want daughters and would resort to female infanticide," he had told me, in a conversation soon after one of the marriages in Shahgang in late '90s.

Interestingly, Shivraj-Sadhna Singh have two sons—Kartikeya and Kunal—and no daughter.

After his ascendency to the Chief Minister's chair in 2005, he converted his personal mission into a policy and launched a massive campaign for women empowerment, Beti Bachao Abhiyan (save the girl child) and the Laadli Laxmi Yojana. "I had my own limitation — how much could I have done with my limited resources and in

## 90  *Shivraj Singh And Rise Of Madhya Pradesh*

a small place like Vidisha…the message required to go all over the state as it was in everyone's interest," he explained.

According to a recent document submitted before the 14th Finance Commission (that visited Madhya Pradesh in February 2014) detailing the plan outlays in major schemes for women, there are 21 schemes—highest ever— being run by the State's Women & Child Development Department, Agriculture Department (promoting participation of women in agriculture), Higher Education Department, Social Justice Department, Scheduled Caste Welfare Department and Tribal Welfare Department and so on in MP.

Ladli Laxmi Yojana, launched in 2006, was to essentially tackle issues relating to female infanticide, marriage of minor girls and education of girls. He knew the psyche of most of the uneducated poor villagers who treated a girl child as an unwanted burden. So Shivraj tried to convert the burden into a celebration and this happened through several policy interventions—again because of his own personal experiences in his rural surroundings.

The girl child issue, the illegal infanticide cases and the skewed child sex ratio have been problems at the national level too. Most of the states including progressive states like Maharashtra have been grappling with it. The legal interventions by governments such as strict actions under the stringent PC & PNDT Act (Pre-Conception and Pre-Natal Diagnostic Techniques Act), provisions against medical practitioners and gynaecologists involved in sex determination cases and operations did not help. From Bhopal only one doctor has been jailed so far in the past 15 years. The Swagatam Laxmi Yojana was started very recently for effective implementation of the Act, after the 2013 elections that returned Shivraj with a massive majority—close to 72% women reportedly voted for Shivraj, the sole star campaigner in the elections.

In Madhya Pradesh, the northern region of Gwalior (840/1000), and Morena (829/1000) districts had the worst child sex ratios. Adjoining districts of Bhind (843/1000) and Datia (856/1000)—all in the Gwalior-Chambal region—also offered the same challenges to policy makers for many years. The patriarchal social set up has been the prime reason of female foeticide and infanticide cases in these areas, besides lack of awareness.

Shivraj was of the opinion that only penal actions were not the solution to such a widely prevalent and deep-rooted social issue. Women empowerment and education, besides addressing their basic issues was the need of the hour. The aggressive campaign to save a girl child got Shivraj a nick-name across the state as their *Mama* (maternal uncle). In his speeches he would assure girls "don't worry about your education, don't worry about marriage and deliveries…. your *Mama* is here to look after you." There was therefore an extraordinary stress on implementation by bureaucracy of schemes for girls and women as his '*Mama*' image travelled far and wide. He was genuinely concerned about the future of women and girls. Schemes like free bicycles, school uniforms, free education up to certain standards and other schemes have been tried by other State Governments to promote education but Shivraj Government's social objective was altogether different.

By launching the Beti Bachao Campaign (Save Girl Child) on 5 October 2011 he tried to create an atmosphere all over the State that the government was all for girls and women. While MP became the first state in the country which went out of its way to launch a campaign for the safety of the newly-born girl child, it also became the first state where pension was provided to parents crossing 60 years of age, having only daughters. According to Census 2011, the child sex ratio that was 932/1000 in 2001, went down to 918/1000 in 2011, a dip of 14 points, drawing the government's immediate attention.

In Madhya Pradesh, independent and departmental efforts to improve the sex ratio have been quite dismal.

Under the Ladli Laxmi Yojana, the MP Government purchases National Savings Certificates worth ₹ 6,000 annually for five years after a girl is born into a family. A certain portion of the money is also made available for her education. "At the age of 21, if the girl has not married before 18 years of age, a lump sum of ₹ 1.18 lakh is given to her," said a top official from the Women and Child Development Department, who said close to 15 lakh girls have been benefited so far through this scheme. The purpose of the scheme was to promote educational and socio-economic status of the girl child across MP.

It was not only about the arrival of a girl into this world but as per Shivraj's plan, his government sensitised the entire official machinery and introduced gender budgeting in 2007-08 to assess gender-wise allocation of resources and impact of policies and programmes on gender disparities. Initially it was limited to 13 departments but now 25 departments are covered. Gender budgeting is an imported concept, implemented by Australia and South Africa in the '90s, with the United Nations Development Programme (UNDP) with Union Women and Child Development Ministry issuing guidelines for the same later.

This was followed by Women's Policy in August 2008, as was required under the 12 Five Year Plan of the Government of India. The aim was to ensure total and dignified participation of women in

Social Concerns 93

the development process and integrating them with the mainstream of development.

What Shivraj had undertaken as his own personal mission of helping a poor girl tie the nuptial knot, in the government he converted this into a kind of mandatory scheme called 'Mukhyamantri Kanyadan Yojana and Mukhyamantri Nikah Yojana' for Hindu and Muslim girls, respectively. In the past few years, close to three lakh marriages have been solemnised with an assistance between ₹ 10,000 and 15,000 per girl for the marriage expenses plus for buying household items for the newly-weds.

The difference between any other BJP Chief Minister and Shivraj is that, despite his RSS background and affiliation with Hindu organisations, once in government he has shown equality in letter and spirit for Hindu and Muslim families. If the Kanyadan Yojana was meant for Hindu girls, care was taken to include the Muslim girls and families as well.

Girls of marriageable age from poor families, widows and abandoned women were also covered under the scheme which was quite broad-based. Interestingly, statutory Panchayat bodies, urban bodies and other government agencies were authorised to organise mass marriages to help institutionalise the whole process.

'Sashakta Nari-Sashakta Pradesh' (empowered woman-empowered state) was another slogan he gave while publicly taking oath. He wanted all the male citizens of the State to protect the dignity of women in every sense of the term. The government's scheme 'Sabala' has so far benefited eight lakh girls and institutional deliveries created a sort of record wherein 64 lakh women have delivered babies in government hospitals over the last few years. In other words, in 2003 the institutional deliveries were 26% which grew to 84%, while in the corresponding period, as many as 9,000 beds in government hospitals were increased to facilitate deliveries.

This particular chapter on governance may appear to be heavily loaded with official figures as well as schemes but my idea was only to highlight how a leader, from a modest rural background, drawing upon his personal experiences, could bring about a change in the mindset at the highest level of bureaucracy and infuse a sense of responsibility towards the women and girl children in an otherwise insensitive government machinery. The framing of policies in a large number and providing direct benefits to girls and women was otherwise not feasible under normal governance practices.

This does not at all mean that the sex ratio has improved overnight or crimes against women have gone down to zero in Madhya Pradesh. But with sincere efforts such as 50% reservation for women in local bodies—there are close to 1.50 lakh women who have occupied posts from a *panch* to a Mayor because of these reservations, the awareness of women has grown side by side with their education.

The State Government in its presentation before the Finance Commission conceded: "poor nutritional status and high crime rate against women in MP are still the areas of concern."

My endeavour is to highlight the quality of political leadership provided by Shivraj Singh who thinks of social concerns and comes up with a set of schemes and solutions, while still busy in turning around the economic scenario of the state through agriculture and industrialisation.

CRCRCR

Chapter - 8

# THE SPORTS BUFF

During the last World Cup Cricket Championship that India won, a few journalists got a surprise call from the Chief Minister's house to come over. Nothing was conveyed as to why they were being invited. Nonetheless, a group of selected journalists hoping to get a scoop—something which is otherwise difficult to extract from Shivraj Singh—reached his Shyamla Hills residence. A crucial game involving India was to be played in the afternoon. When the journalists reached the hall where the CM normally meets visitors, a slim man attired in a navy blue track suit and wearing a sports cap was receiving the visitors. The journalists could not recognise this man. Most of the staff of the CM house is familiar to the journalists who visit it frequently. So they thought he was perhaps a new member of the staff in the CM house.

Well, he was none other than the Chief Minister himself, personally receiving the scribes to enjoy the live telecast of the one-day international between India and South Africa, at his home, over cups of tea and refreshments. He wanted to watch the game with friends like us and had created a sporting atmosphere in the hall; he was dressed for the occasion too. If I recollect rightly, it was 12 March 2011 and the game India was playing was at Nagpur. Dhoni's

96  *Shivraj Singh And Rise Of Madhya Pradesh*

brigade lost by three wickets. But it was a unique experience for the journalists covering the political beat. The CM could have easily watched the game with his personal friends and family members. By collecting a few journalists, he did not intend to influence them in any way. It was a simple gesture on his part to spend some quality time chit-chatting with journalists on sports and related subjects while watching cricket.

Shivraj had played cricket, volleyball, kabaddi and football at his school and college in the '70s, though not at a higher competitive level, given his modest rural background and upbringing. But he is a keen sports lover, unlike those who take 'interest' in a particular game for the sake of grabbing a post in sports bodies and helping themselves rather than the sport or its players.

Incidentally, in India a large number of politicians and chief ministers with different political affiliations have been the presidents or chairmen of various sports bodies. Vijay Kumar Malhotra (BJP) is among the oldest of politicians to have been associated with a sport (archery) which was a less popular discipline in the '80s. He then got entry into the Indian Olympic Association (IOA) as well. I remember having interviewed him as a sports correspondent at the *Free Press Journal* (FPJ), way back in 1984-85 when a BJP working committee meeting was held in Indore and Malhotra had come from Delhi. Then there have been Lalu Yadav, Arun Jaitley, Farooq Abdullah, late Madhavrao Scindia, his son Jyotiraditya, Narendra Modi, late Vilasrao Deshmukh, Rajiv Shukla, Sharad Pawar—all associated with cricket in one capacity or the other at some point of time in their political career. Other prominent names of past and present include Priya Ranjan Dasmunshi and Praful Patel (football), Natwar Singh (lawn tennis), late Vasant Sathe (badminton), Vitthalrao Gadgil (kho kho), Ajit Pawar (kabaddi), late KC Pant (fencing), KP Singhdeo (rowing), and Abhay Chautala (boxing). Late Vidya Charan Shukla was perhaps the first of the lot to have entered the sports arena from politics. For decades, he headed the SNIPES (Society of National Institutes of Physical Education and Sports) which later became the All-India Council of Sports (AICS). Eventually, he took over as the big daddy of the IOA where he entered as the Badminton Association of India (BAI) chief. He was credited with reviving the National Games in 1985 in Delhi. Sharad Pawar's former aide Suresh Kalmadi, the Congress MP from Pune who succeeded Shukla in mid-eighties, remained for long the boss of All India Athletics Federation (AIAF) and then the IOA. After being jailed for Commonwealth Games corruption, he lost both the positions and is almost out of the sports arena now.

Having been associated with sports myself for many years, I know that not all politicians crave for control of sports bodies. KC Pant, Deputy Chairman of the Planning Commission, was president of the Fencing Federation of India. When I tried to speak with him about the plans to promote the sport in the country, he gave me a blank look and then took me aside at the Daly College, Indore, in the late '80s and asked, "Who told you that I am the president?" For a moment I was aghast, but then picked up courage (being a junior sports correspondent that I was then) to confidently say, "Yes, I know you are holding the post." It was then that the affable Pant muttered a few words and said, "I am looking for the person who has made me the president, I don't know how come I have been nominated to the Federation. If you come to know, please do let me know," were his parting words. The person who had nominated him without Pant's consent was a seasoned sports organiser from Jabalpur, I later found out.

The same was the case with Madhavrao Scindia who took over

## 98 *Shivraj Singh And Rise Of Madhya Pradesh*

as the president of the MP Cricket Association (MPCA) in 1982-83 with much reluctance. The Indore-headquartered MPCA's activities were being run by AW Kanmadikar in the '70s. Satish Malhotra, a prominent Mumbai businessman and husband of Indore's Maharani Usha Devi (Holkar), was the president of the MPCA and had quit his post after contributing a few years to the association. Cricket did not have the big money that it has today. Conducting coaching camps and sending teams for Ranji Trophy National Championships was difficult those days. So Kanmadikar, who later became the BCCI secretary, contacted a reluctant scion of the Gwalior royal family through Malhotra and convinced him to head the MPCA. Many years later Kanmadikar told me, "Unless you have an influential person with you, local administration officials do not listen to you even for small things required to organise an event."

Almost the same thing happened with his son when senior Scindia died in a plane crash in September 2001 and the MPCA was rendered headless. Indore's cricket administrators and former players persuaded Jyotiraditya Scindia to take over, first as the chairman and then as the president. Digvijay Singh, as CM, had then extended a helping hand to junior Scindia to enter the MPCA. Digvijay himself was a good cricketer as a student of Daly College and later at the engineering college, SGSITS, Indore, besides being a fine squash player. He, however, did not become a part-time sports administrator.

But that cannot be said of veteran politician Sharad Pawar whose greed to hold on to cricket-associated power seems never ending. After he served a full term as chairman of the BCCI and then the International Cricket Council (ICC), he once again fought elections of the Bombay Cricket Association (BCA) recently and won. Immediately before that the NCP supremo had put up Vilasrao

Deshmukh, a former CM of Maharashtra from the Congress, to stall the entry of ex-Indian skipper Dilip Vengsarkar into the BCA. The polling saw a politician beat a cricketer, with all the money power at the former's disposal.

This brief overall view of country's sports administration pattern was necessary to enlighten the reader about what has been happening in the sporting world of Madhya Pradesh for the past few years. Now there is a Chief Minister taking interest in sports without being involved in it directly for any gain whatsoever. I have attended a number of sports award functions in Bhopal and Indore and have clearly felt Shivraj's genuine love for sports and sportspersons.

## Setting New Records

Ranchi's National Games (2011) was a red-letter event in MP's sports history. Madhya Pradesh players performed exceedingly well. They picked up as many as 102 medals (25-gold; 32-silver; 46-bronze). Though Manipur, Haryana and Maharashtra were ahead of MP, the sporting world of the country sat up and took notice of MP which was emerging as a solid sporting power. In the earlier version of the games at Guwahati in 2007, MP athletes had shone marginally to bag 63 medals in different disciplines. But the performance prior to Guwahati was very dismal, matching a typical BIMARU state, if I may borrow the demographic term and apply it to sports.

Economic conditions in the country were generally looking up compared to the days of pre-globalisation and monetary flow had improved in private as well as government sectors. Sponsors were easier to find than in the past. The sportsmen in MP too were happy with the higher monetary gains and recognition, thanks to a series of steps taken to promote sports culture across the state by the government. The 'playing population', as they say in sports terminology, grew steadily over the years with so many incentives.

Is running sports activities a government's job ? This debate is very old. So it would not be out of place to ask whether a government should regulate sports or not. Also, to what extent should sports administrators be allowed to hold on to a position. There was a Sports Bill proposed by the Central Government that brought in many new measures but the sports federations opposed it. In the '90s there were 'guidelines' brought in by the Sports Authority of India. All this had given birth to bitter controversies and sports did not benefit much from it.

Madhya Pradesh could somehow keep itself insulated from the unseemly controversies at the national level and inched slowly towards bettering results.

The first thing the Sports and Youth Welfare Department in MP did was to regularise the pending state sports awards, known as Vikram Awards. Before 2007, they were not distributed for years together and this had a dampening effect on the sportsmen. With the regularisation of awards functions, and preceding that, the proper selections by a competent jury, young players got tremendous motivation. At the first awards function, Shivraj Singh announced government jobs for all Vikram awardees straightaway. Close to 60-65 players got jobs. The State Government already had a jobs scheme for the meritorious players. There are currently three main awards which are conferred upon the sportsmen and coaches after achieving a certain eligibility—Vikram, Vishwamitra (to a coach) and Eklavya (junior player). The cash prize that these awards carried was ₹ 50,000 for the first two categories and ₹ 25,000 for the junior category. All have been doubled by the Shivraj government. Now a Vikram awardee takes home a hefty rupees one lakh, just like the Shiv Chhatrapati Awards of Maharashtra.

The sports budget which was a paltry six crore in 2005, rose to ₹130 crore in 2013 and with this quantum jump the number of sports activities and sportsmen also started growing. Sports in Madhya Pradesh are no longer confined to big cities like Indore, Bhopal, Gwalior or Jabalpur but have spread to every nook and corner of the state with academies opened up in Seoni, Betul and even in the tribal Naxal-infested belt of Balaghat.

As many as 17 sports coaching academies are now functioning in the state for sports like cricket, wrestling, badminton, hockey (women's hockey in Gwalior and men's in Bhopal), judo, taekwondo, wushu, karate, equestrian, shooting, fencing, water sports, archery and boxing. It was the wushu squad trained at the academy at Bhopal which had won the most medals in Ranchi's National Games, the last held so far. The karate team of MP has become the national champions in 2014 for the first time.

Dr Shailendra Shrivastava, IPS, Director of Sports and Youth Welfare, told me, "The net result of various steps taken in the last 6-7 years by me and my predecessor (Sanjay Chaudhary), was the quantum jump in playing population of MP. Department of Youth Welfare alone draws 10-15 lakh players annually in its different competitions, a figure which was earlier in a few thousands." He says that state sports bodies' players are different which would take the playing population to a much higher level. Dr Shrivastava during his short stint bagged three awards: Admiral Kohli Award for promoting yachting, from the Yachting Federation of India; E-Governance Award 2012 by the GoI for excellence in sports through innovative use of ICT (optimum coverage of athletes' performance enhancing technologies and reducing injuries) while the third one came from Population First and UNFPA for best campaign on girl child (Hum Chhunyenge Aasman) to promote sports among girls. Shrivastava says constant guidance and monitoring from the Chief Minister was the most encouraging factor for the department and the players.

Shivraj Singh shot into sporting fame when he on his own announced an unprecedented rupees one crore grant to the women hockey players who were not from his state. They were undergoing training at the Sports Authority of India's (SAI) advanced coaching centre at Bhopal but were facing financial problems. He followed it up with the same grant to the men's team which was preparing for the London Olympic Games of 2012. What was significant in this was that most of the players did not belong to MP but since they were being ill-treated by the warring groups of Hockey India and the Government of India's Sports Ministry, Shivraj utilised the opportunity to sincerely help the players from the coffers of his state.

"I was feeling bad while reading in newspapers that despite it being our national game, hockey was hugely neglected." Shivraj had told this to his Sports Director Sanjay Chaudhary, an IPS officer, who converted Shivraj's vision into reality over the five years he was at the helm of affairs. It was Chaudhary's long stint that gave a much-needed fillip to sports in MP. The CM called the women hockey players to his house, felicitated them and gave cheques to each member of the team. This was like a windfall, as the players had never ever expected the MP government to bother about their plight, let alone come forward to financially help them as they belonged to various other states like Punjab, Himachal, West Bengal and Maharashtra.

In Madhya Pradesh, the post of the Director Sports has been with the IPS officers since 1985-86 when Yatish Chandra, a DIG, became the first Director Sports under Motilal Vora's government. That year President Giani Zail Singh was the chief guest at the Vikram Award ceremony at Indore. Motilal Vora, like many of

## The Sports Buff 103

Shivraj's predecessors, had no interest in sports. Once I was in the car with Chief Minister Vora and Railways Minister Madhavrao Scindia, taking them to the sports ground of Indore's famous sports club of yore, Happy Wanderers. The sports ground was being taken over under a government scheme and the players were agitated. They belonged to the lower middle class and had only one field to play on in the heart of the city. They had sought immediate intervention from the CM but Vora neither understood the case nor felt like visiting the ground to pacify the agitated players. The playground was finally taken over for a road construction scheme with players' problems going unheard.

But times have changed in today's Madhya Pradesh. The government has completely transformed the scenario. The sports infrastructure is superb; scholarships, rewards and jobs for the players are guaranteed and for world class training a number of academies, equipped with latest sports technology, are giving round-the-clock training. Coaches like Ashok Dhyanchand (hockey), Olympian Sushil Kumar (wrestling), Madanlal (cricket), P Gopichand (badminton) and Mansher Singh (shooting) have been hired on decent salaries to impart coaching to MP boys and girls. In all, 11 hockey astro-turfs are being laid across MP.

The astro-turfs remind me of KPS Gill, the haughty president of the Indian Hockey Federation (IHF) and former DGP of Punjab. He won a one-sided election to the IHF post at its annual general body meeting held in Bhopal in 1995 beating Ghufran Azam, the then a vice-president of IHF. To prevent the Congress muscleman from Bhopal, a lobby within the federation had propped up Gill, with his fame as the super cop who had stamped out terrorism in Punjab. Soon after his victory Gill, twirling his moustache proudly, had announced at a heavily guarded press conference of the Lake

View Ashoka Hotel, that he would lay down 100 astro-turfs all over the country. Unfortunately, even 10% could not be laid during his tenure as the boss of Indian hockey. In my opinion Gill did more damage to hockey than good.

Luckily, in MP, after Yatish Chandra, the post remained with IPS officials throughout and Chaudhary was replaced by Dr Shailendra Shrivastava who was an IG, sometime in 2011-12. Most of them served sports, unlike the former DGP of Punjab. With an IPS official at the helms of affairs, many things fall in place for players and that is being experienced by sportsmen in MP.

As mentioned earlier, Shivraj is devoted to sports. He does not get into any controversy involving sports. This was witnessed in MP at least twice. The MP Cricket Association (MPCA) is a prestigious body having its own beautiful stadium at Indore. One of Shivraj's Cabinet ministers from Indore, Kaliash Vijayvargiya, wanted to capture the sports body and with his clout, muscle and money power entered the fray. The MPCA had a tradition of consensus. It never had elections and the association was running peacefully. But with Vijayvargiya, the then industries minister, throwing his hat in the ring, there was a tough contest between him and Congress leader and MPCA president Jyotiraditya Scindia who had mobilised huge funds for a flood-lit stadium in Indore. This is now complete and another is being built in Gwalior—both ODI venues recognised by the Board of Control for Cricket in India since long. The cricket atmosphere in Indore got vitiated due to the stand-off between these two politicians. With the image that he has, Vijayvargiya's very name was enough of a threat to the white-collared members of the MPCA. He challenged a well-mannered Scindia twice in the biennial elections to the MPCA and lost on both occasions. Indore had a rich legacy of top cricketers and it was once the cricket capital of

India, with players such as CK Nayudu, Chandu Sarwate, Mushtaq Ali, JN Bhaya, CS Nayudu, MM Jagdale and others winning Ranji Championships for the Holkars team. But an ambitious politician left a bad taste in the mouths of Indore's cricket loving people as he tried to misuse his power to the hilt. Cases were filed in High Court and so on. MP High Court, Indore Bench had to sit on a Sunday to decide the case of some members.

It was to Shivraj's credit that he did not join the issue at all and remained independent on both occasions. If he had wished, he could have created problems for the Congress leader Scindia and favoured his own Cabinet colleague.

But Shivraj Singh says that he loves to play straight—be it sports or politics. In sports, he does not bring in politics and in politics, he takes things sportingly. And this is how he has always been.

ଓଓଓଓ

Chapter - 9

# BUREAUCRACY, CRIME AND CORRUPTION

Democracy and development must go hand in hand. If development is stalled, people lose faith in democracy. But ideally under any form of governance growth must match the aspirations of those governed. Good governance is best possible in a corruption-free society. But if corruption and irregularities flourish, timely and effective punishment is the only way to keep things in check.

Kautilya—also known as Chanakya—in his epochal treatise *Arthashastra* (Economics) had, many centuries ago, elaborated on a system of penalties prescribed under the Kautilyan state. *Arthashastra* is therefore also known as *dandaniti*—policy of punishment. Rulers awarded punishments to help maintain social order; to prevent misconduct by civil servants, including exploitation of the public and causing revenue loss to the state and to avoid dissatisfaction, rebellions or revolts.

Times have changed since Kautilya envisaged an ideal state. However, people's expectations from rulers, both political and bureaucratic, remain unchanged. The single most important expectation in 21st century seems to be control of corruption, whether through sterner enforcement of existing laws or through a new Lokpal institution or something else. Many would agree that the Lokayukta institutions in the states have worked well only if the individuals heading them were above board and had the will to take on people in high places.

The phenomenon of corruption has always had multiple facets. I know of people in business houses who grease the palms of politicians, officials and others to get their work speeded up—paying to cut the red tape.

But times are changing. There is much greater awareness in the civil society today to fight corruption. Governments are under pressure to do something drastic. We may call it the Anna Hazare effect! People across India are yearning for upright politicians as well as civil servants who can deliver good governance so that the masses live peacefully and happily and achieve overall growth.

The growing decadence in society however makes one wonder if this will ever happen in India. In some areas we see hope while in others, we don't. The performance of UPA-II is a pointer to lack of good governance and thriving of corruption. The aspirations of the common man have been trampled upon or ignored.

In Madhya Pradesh under Shivraj Singh's rule, corruption may not have been stamped out totally nor perhaps will it ever be—but the beginnings of good governance practices are evident all around. This is also the reason why the BJP was voted back to power for the third time in a row with a massive majority. This was clearly not the case during the Digvijay Singh regime. He spoke of good governance but only to pay lip service.

If we presume that bureaucrats (IAS, IPS, IFS officials and numerous State services officials, as also engineers working in the construction departments like PWD, irrigation, PHE etc) are fairly honest and the set of politicians ruling over them are dishonest or inefficient, the opposite of this also holds equally good!

Politicians, especially the tribe that has lately been in power, seldom get along with bureaucrats who are upright and rule-bound. A running battle between politicians and officers is seen in many states where parties of different hues and ideologies have enjoyed power—Ashok Khemka in Haryana or a Durga Shakti Nagpal in UP or an Arun Bhatia, (retired) in Maharashtra—all of them, IAS officers, had problems with their political bosses due to their personal integrity and conviction. There are IPS officials who have suffered due to their being upright. There were others like Vijay Pandhre, a chief engineer who exposed the multi-crore scam in the NCP-led irrigation department in Maharashtra last year. While he retired, a former water expert, Madhavrao Chitale of Aurangabad (ex-secretary, Government of India's Water Resources Department) was entrusted with the responsibility of probing the irregularities. The one-man commission submitted its report after more than a year, though the findings were not out till end of February, 2014. There are many more such daring officers at different levels—unsung heroes of our time—not just from the elite IAS and IPS services, who refuse to bow down to corrupt politicians. Sadly, their percentage is steadily dwindling with the fast changing value system. Bollywood superstar Aamir Khan, in an informal chat with the author on the eve of the second 'Satyamev Jayate' series said, "It seems everyone is chasing money as if nothing is left to be done in society."

However, a number of pliable officers are also there in each system working hand in glove with politicians who rake-off big money at the cost of the people. If 'all is well', the system works smoothly, much to the disadvantage of the hapless people. This was evident in the huge corruption in MP by the couple, Arvind and Tinoo Joshi (both IAS officers) who kept defrauding the system

## 110 *Shivraj Singh And Rise Of Madhya Pradesh*

to make big money with the connivance or collusion of successive politicians in different departments and ministries in Bhopal and Delhi.

If either a bureaucrat or a politician refuses to walk the unethical path and takes the right stand, the working relationship between the two gets disturbed. Policies can't be implemented in the given time frame. The blow-hot, blow-cold relationship between the legislature and the executive is one of the notable peculiarities of the Indian democratic set-up.

## Controlling The Bureaucracy

Ironically, my friends in politics often tell me that controlling the bureaucracy is like riding a stubborn horse… it will behave the way you want it to, if the rider is skilled enough, tough and experienced. I do not quote this opinion here to glorify Indian politicians nor do I wish to undermine the role of bureaucracy. There have been outstanding politicians as well as outstanding administrators in our country. But several events in many states, as also in the Government of India, in the past few decades, have exposed the inherent shortcomings on both sides, causing deep resentment among people. Umpteen examples can be cited in support of this argument.

This chapter deals with the challenges faced by Shivraj Singh in MP while dealing with crime and corruption either in bureaucracy or in society or within his own party, besides touching on the law and order situation during the past eight years.

Within three months of assuming power for the first time, Shivraj had to take a tough call regarding the head of the State's bureaucracy. One IAS officer did not perhaps act the way his government wanted him to. He was Vijay Singh, otherwise a dynamic and upright officer of the MP cadre. But he was removed by Shivraj Singh in a swift move that surprised many outside the bureaucracy and sent shock waves within the *babudom*. A 1970-batch officer, Singh was Chief Secretary of Madhya Pradesh for just about a year, before being suddenly dumped into the Revenue Board (Gwalior), as its chairman. This had created ripples in the State in early 2006 as it was the first major decision of the Shivraj Government that caught the public's eye. The Chief Secretary was held responsible for trying to protect an IAS officer SR Mohanty who was involved in a scam. Vijay Singh had an elite background. His father, LP Singh was an ICS officer of 1935 batch and had also served as the Union Home Secretary under Prime Minister Lal Bahadur Shastri. Vijay Singh was quite urbane, handsome and an impressive bureaucrat. His refined mannerisms, good command over the English language and commanding personality had earned him a distinct standing in MP. I can claim to have had a fairly good professional relationship with him since his stint at Indore as the Divisional Commissioner in early '90s. He had one shortcoming—he trusted his officers blindly. Many tainted officers could thus get closer to him and extract 'good' postings. If he found himself in trouble despite all his good qualities it was due to this singular trait. He incurred Shivraj Singh's ire for not informing him about a reference made in an affidavit to the High Court through Advocate General RN Singh about Mohanty, one of the accused in the ₹ 719 crore Inter-corporate deposit scam. After a few months of his removal from MP, Singh became the country's Defence Secretary and retired from there.

But then Singh was not the first such officer. There has been a history of sorts in MP when Chief Secretaries were not only removed but even suspended. Arjun Singh, who lorded over the state as CM (1980-1985), before Prime Minister Rajiv Gandhi shunted him to the trouble-torn Punjab as Governor, had the 'distinction' of

## 112 Shivraj Singh And Rise Of Madhya Pradesh

punishing two Chief Secretaries. The first was BK Dube (6 March 1980-29 October 1980) whom Arjun Singh suspended soon after assuming power, for 'conspiring' against the CM (a fact never proved). It is of course the CM's prerogative to choose any officer to head the bureaucracy, so he exercised his powers and brought in G Jagathpathy. Again in 1982, Singh had serious differences with another Chief Secretary, Birbal, whom Singh himself had made the Chief Secretary in August 1982. Birbal was summarily removed in May 1983 for reasons best known to the politician who is no more now. Some former bureaucrats say he was replaced as he was ineffective in leading the administration.

There is, however, a vast difference between Arjun Singh and Shivraj Singh's style of functioning. Bureaucrats used to be quite fearful of Arjun Singh. He also had the reputation of being a very shrewd politician but not transparent as an individual. One can say he was a very private person. During Shivraj's tenure—20 years down the line, things have changed a lot, in society, in politics and in the bureaucracy. The fear factor has come down considerably among officials, for various reasons, including Shivraj's easy-going behaviour and nature. His body language and overall personality gels with the common man. He seldom speaks English, but is a well-read politician. He does not evoke fear. He is shrewd but not cunning.

Rakesh Sahani, a 1972 batch IAS officer and a former Delhi IITian (who was picked to succeed Vijay Singh as CS after superceding many officers senior to him), is credited for the success that Shivraj Singh got in the initial years, including the Assembly polls victory in 2008. If Shivraj could settle down in his job at a crucial time and concentrate on people-oriented policies, it was due to Sahani and CM's Principal Secretary Iqbal Singh Bains, now posted in Delhi. Sahani was handpicked by Shivraj after consultation

## Bureaucracy, Crime and Corruption 113

with Sunderlal Patwa and others, when stability was badly required as the entire bureaucracy was stunned and appeared directionless after the sudden departure of Singh.

Shivraj's gamble paid off as Sahani was a hands-on bureaucrat with excellent grasp of a wide range of subjects. A hard-worker and an astute administrator, he was fully trusted by Shivraj for all the four years that he headed the bureaucracy, a fact Sushma Swaraj, the MP from Vidisha and Leader of Opposition in the Lok Sabha, acknowledged while informally talking to me at Bhopal soon after her party's 2013 victory. I had asked her the secret of Shivraj's success to which she had said, "Picking up the right people for right posts and getting things done in time." Despite defending Vijay Singh in the affidavit matter of the ICD scam, Sahani, on his part, did not promote Mohanty when the 1982 batch of the IAS got promoted to the Principal Secretary's grade in 2007 in MP, pending enquiries. Mohanty, surprisingly got a 'provisional and conditional promotion' in 2012 with retrospective effect from February 2007 through R Parashuram, the then Chief Secretary. The promotion was subject to different clearances from departmental enquiry, the court and Department of Personnel and Training, GoI, as was mentioned in the first of its kind order (No: E-1/464/2011/5/1). A former Chief Secretary wondered how such a conditional promotion could be given to any IAS officer, for there was no provision in the rules, according to him.

In Vijay Singh's case, Shivraj was right in that a politically sensitive scam involving crores of rupees of the State Government undertaking, and the one his party's CM Uma Bharti had exposed (possibly to fix Digvijay Singh), should have been brought to his notice. Since the High Court granted SR Mohanty, main accused in the scam, the much-needed relief, the case eventually got weakened.

114  *Shivraj Singh And Rise Of Madhya Pradesh*

There was also a political dimension to it. Prahlad Patel, former MP and general secretary of Uma Bharti's Bhartiya Janshakti Party, had threatened to sit on dharna in Bhopal, in the first week of January, following the sudden resignation of the Advocate General Singh who was accused of supporting Mohanty on the Chief Secretary's intervention in the same case. Uma Bharti had considered handing over the case to the CBI but by then the NDA led by Vajpayee, had lost power to the UPA and Manmohan Singh as PM had taken over in Delhi. A number of IAS officials were directly or indirectly involved in the scam as they had served on the board of the corporation in different capacities at different times. Mohanty, a fairly resourceful officer, succeeded in getting the FIR quashed from the High Court with a friendly affidavit from the state government. However it put a lasting blot on Vijay Singh's otherwise spotless career.

*The Hindu, Indian Express* and *Hindustan Times* had extensively written about the scam. Two industrialist brothers who could not pay back the loan of the MPSIDC were sentenced to jail recently.

But Vijay Singh was not the only top official who faced the wrath of Shivraj Singh. A year later, in an equally dramatic move, Shivraj sacked the Director General of Police, Swaraj Puri, IPS, in September, 2006.

The reasons for the removal of the two top bureaucrats—IAS and IPS—were entirely different but they established Shivraj's credentials as a tough administrator at a time when people in the State generally speculated that he was also a stop-gap CM like his predecessors—Uma Bharti and Babulal Gaur, who were replaced in quick succession.

The reputation of the two officers and their backgrounds were not the same. The only similarity between the two was that both had been appointed by Babulal Gaur, and in the appointment of Puri as DGP, Chief Secretary Singh had played an important role.

Bureaucracy, Crime and Corruption 115

These two actions portrayed him as one who exposed the wrong-doings in high places. Though new to the job, Shivraj let everyone know that he had arrived and would not tolerate any kind of corruption. Now well after eight years into his job, with three feathers in his chief ministerial cap, Shivraj is still dealing with the corrupt officials (and ministers) with a degree of firmness. Upon his return, he spoke of zero tolerance for corruption during his swearing-in ceremony.

In his first interview granted to *Dainik Bhaskar* after his first victory in 2008 Assembly polls, as CM, he had categorically told me (the interviewer) that though complete stamping out of corruption was difficult due to multiple challenges, it was his priority. Accordingly, he placed Health Director Rajesh Rajora, an IAS officer, under suspension again after an Income Tax raid on the health department officials and also dropped Health Minister Ajay Vishnoi from his cabinet. That the Lokayukta later cleared both is a different story.

However, the biggest blow to MP's bureaucracy and political establishment was delivered by the IAS couple, Arvind Joshi and Tinoo Joshi. They gave Shivraj some sleepless nights. That was one case which rocked the bureaucracy all over the country with amazing amounts of black money tumbling out of Joshis' cupboards. It gave a bad name to MP, in general. They were trapped by the Income Tax Department after a raid on their official residence in Bhopal's posh locality. The Joshis were accused of amassing assets disproportionate to their known sources of income. They were also held for corrupt practices. The CM did not take much time to put them under suspension in 2010 and later with the consent of the GoI—they being all-India service officers—terminated their services. Both were IAS officers of principal secretaries' rank and belonged to the 1979 batch. According to a lengthy report in the *Indian Express*, the Lokayukta's Special Police Establishment (SPE) unearthed ₹ 43.20 crore from them, though Income Tax authorities, according to the paper, claimed unspecified assets in excess of ₹ 360 crore from the couple. When the raid took place, ₹ 3.04 crore in cash was recovered from Arvind Joshi's D-19, 74-Bungalow where the Ministers and IAS officers reside in Bhopal.

There are many who point to the ever-rising corruption in MP and feel the CM is not doing enough to curb corruption with an iron hand. The Professional Examination Board (Vyapam) recruitment and examination scandal having serious ramifications for the medical education system, played out fully before the public on the eve of the November 2013 elections. Lakshmi Kant Sharma, the Technical Education Minister once close to the CM and the RSS, was neck-deep in it and the State police's Special Task Force (STF) had acted against him. His defeat in the election in November from Sironj, in Vidisha district, simplified the police's job but he was not arrested like many others.

## Swaraj Puri Case

As far as Swaraj Puri is concerned, he was removed the next day after the Economic Offences Wing (EOW) registered a case against him under sections 420, 468 and 471 of IPC for allegedly forging documents to get his son admitted to an engineering college of Indore under the NRI quota. The case did not stand in court eventually much to the relief of Puri but he lost the top cop's job that he had got after much effort.

Puri is the same IPS official who was Superintendent of Police of Bhopal when the worst industrial disaster took place, killing thousands due to inhaling of the deadly MiC gas that leaked at midnight from Union Carbide factory in December 1984. He worked the whole night and the next few days, helping the gas victims but ended up being a victim himself. He was charged with letting US citizen Warren Anderson, the UCIL chairman, flee from Bhopal, in the SP's official car. When this fact came to light well after Puri's retirement, around the 28 anniversary of the gas disaster, he was removed again by Shivraj Singh from a sinecure post-retirement job he was holding in the State Government.

During the Lok Sabha elections in 2009, I was on a campaign trail to different parts of the state travelling with Shivraj. Among various political topics, we also got talking about the law and order situation, crime rate and so on. Two successive communal riots in Indore and in Burhanpur were just a year old in which eight and nine people had been killed, respectively. I was generally asking him about the crime rate going up in MP, especially in Bhopal where gold chain snatching had become a routine affair and incidences of rapes were increasing. The cases of Singh and Puri also came up for discussion.

At this stage, Shivraj had told me that his personal policy was 'not to frame anyone and not to save anyone'. In other words, he conveyed that he was tough on corruption and other wrong-doings but would not gun for anyone on his own, be it a politician or a bureaucrat. However, if anyone was found guilty, he would not take a minute to punish the errant politician or a clerk, notwithstanding the position he was holding.

This became amply clear when he took stern action against Bhaiyya Raja and his wife Asha Rani Singh (who was BJP's sitting MLA from Bijawar in Chattarpur district of Bundelkhand). Both faced charges of murder and conspiracy to kill a young girl whom Ashok Veer Vikram Singh alias Bhaiyya Raja, the former MLA from

Pawai in Panna district in Bundelkhand had sexually exploited. In his younger days as a politician, Bhaiyya Raja was known for everything that was unlawful, illegal and immoral. Mere mention of his name evoked terror and when the case came to light, many influential Thakur leaders of MP had telephoned the CM to prevent his arrest. "You can understand how much pressure my party, as well as others, were exerting on me to let him go scot-free," the CM told me at his home over a cup of tea, soon after Bhaiyya Raja was jailed. His wife, sitting BJP MLA, got 10 years' rigorous imprisonment, while he was sentenced for life.

The other politically significant case is related to his long-time Finance Minister Raghavji Bhai of Vidisha. The 79 year old politician and former Lok Sabha and Rajya Sabha member was caught in an act of sodomy at his official residence in Char Imli at Bhopal. He had had relations with one of his domestic helps. A BJP worker Shiv Shankar Pateria, once close to Raghavji, released the CD showing him in the 'act' on the eve of the Assembly elections, which put the state government in an extremely embarrassing situation. The CD was available to everyone, with Assembly elections round the corner.

Interestingly, in the local Vidisha politics, Shivraj and Raghavji Bhai never got along well. Yet, Shivraj would give him enough respect. He also gave the state exchequer's keys to the tax practitioner, Raghavji for nine years, before sending him to jail in July 2013, and throwing him out of the cabinet and the party following the disgraceful episode. The CD came out in the open and the police quickly registered a case against the veteran politician. The old man and his wife ran for cover, left his official bungalow and stayed in a nondescript apartment from where the police arrested him and sent to jail. He was booked under section 377 of the IPC and related sections. The CM's orders were clear to the police: Let the law take its own course and quickly.

Before ending the chapter, I would like to briefly mention that Shivraj has always been championing the cause of women and the girl child not only to tom-tom his welfare schemes for them. If official statistics are to be believed, in the year 2000, all India's 12.70% crimes against women used to take place in MP alone. This came down to 7.30% in 2011; the rape percentage also drastically dropped from 22.70% in 2000 to 14% in 2011. Overall crime rate has also shown a positive decline. In 2012, MP was 11th in all-India ranking while Delhi was 4th, Andhra Pradesh was 5th and Rajasthan stood 6th.

Decadal crime rate (calculated on per lakh population), comparably, shot up in other states such as Maharashtra where the growth in crime was recorded at 45% , in Rajasthan 78 %, while Delhi showed a rise of staggering 81%, as against 15.71% in MP between 2003 and 2012.

How did this happen? Shivraj Singh says that if the legal system and police are weak, no government can take on the criminals, especially those attacking and harassing women. "Our government created and sanctioned 30,000 new posts in the police department at different levels in the last 10 years which were just 8,900 (new posts) or so between 1993 and 2003."

And he says, "It's not about creating posts alone... the various requirements of the police were prioritised and included in the budget as a plan-head which was a non-plan item earlier. The Government sanctioned ₹ 73 crore for new infrastructure, arms ammunition requirements under different heads in 2012-13 and hiked it further to ₹ 225 crore in 2013-14."

120 *Shivraj Singh And Rise Of Madhya Pradesh*

Shivraj would not like to just reel off figures. He would want me and the people to believe that the Government also 'concentrated on increasing the conviction rate, which is so crucial at the end of day'.

MP gave capital punishment to 12 men for heinous crimes against women and girls, with other suitable punishment to close to 3000 criminals in 2012 and 2013.

Reforming the police system, injecting confidence in them with measures like building 10,000 houses with the help of HUDCO and modernising the force—all put together resulted in checking the crime to some extent in MP.

## Bhojshala Episode

In the Dhar district, near Indore, a common Hindu-Muslim shrine has been a bone of contention over performing *pooja* and offering *namaz*, especially when the Hindu festival Vasant Panchami falls on Fridays. Bhojshala is now in ruins but once upon a time it was a temple of Saraswati (Vagdevi) but the idol is not there and is said to be in London's museum for many years now. The Archaeological Survey of India (ASI) still protects it as the heritage monument where Hindus perform *pooja* with utmost faith. Maintaining peace on that day becomes a challenging task for the police and the district administration. The first such occasion during Shivraj Singh regime came in 2006 February and then in 2013 when Vasant Panchami fell on a Thursday-Friday (14-15 Feb) as per the Hindu almanac. It caused tension over the timing of the *pooja* and offering *namaz* on Kaamal Moula's *mazar*. There have been communal tensions over this in the past. But on both occasions, the Shivraj administration controlled the situation well. In 2013, he was a more mature CM and did not make Indore's Kailash Vijayvargiya the minister in-charge to oversee the arrangements and ensure peace in the election year. Vijayvargiya was incharge in 2006. This happened following a telephone call by a senior leader from Dhar to the CM to make someone else in charge or there could be problems for his Government. Vijayvargiya enjoyed the reputation of a staunch Hindu leader, as also the one politically unsuitable for Shivraj, despite their old friendship during the BJYM days in the early '90s. So Shivraj sent Indore's Mahendra Hardia, the then Health Minister, to take charge at Dhar and control the situation. Yet, a little trouble took place there—if not a big communal riot—and to keep its fallout under control and keep Hindu forces happy, the CM shifted a few officers from Dhar and Indore.

So politics and bureaucracy do enjoy a relationship; of strange bed fellows!

ଔଔଔଔ

Chapter - 10

# BANISHING THE BIMARU

"So long as your State does not develop, we will continue to have problems in Mumbai," Sharad Pawar, National Congress Party (NCP) supremo, was telling me just before the 2003 state elections in MP, at Bhopal's heritage hotel Jehanuma Palace. "We keep getting three trainloads of people into Mumbai daily from states like MP, Bihar, UP and Rajasthan and one trainload goes back with those unable to get jobs. How can we cope with such a situation? It's not Marathi versus Hindi*wallah* confrontation, but about the lack of development in these populous states I am talking about," he emphatically argued. Coming from a responsible national leader it was not a comment to be taken lightly.

I distinctly remember that the former Maharashtra chief minister known for his progressive thinking did not utter the word BIMARU but he very much meant that. Clearly, he was quite concerned about *'Amchi Mumbai'* but appeared to me equally worried about the leadership issues and problems of MP, as also the other backward states.

As a proud citizen of MP who had travelled far and wide, Pawar's remarks stung me deeply. The journalist in me acknowledged the plain truth he was speaking. Though born in Mumbai and having

## 124 *Shivraj Singh And Rise Of Madhya Pradesh*

studied in Pune, I could understand his angst. I was disturbed too.

Not many people outside the elite circles of policy researchers, economists, demographers and a few bureaucrats, however, may be well-versed with the BIMARU concept or its import. Nor do they bother to delve into it. At best, some might take it as a *bimar* state (meaning 'sick' in Hindi), and leave it at that. But the acronym stood precisely for this when coined in the mid-eighties. In the dialect of eastern Uttar Pradesh a sick person is often called *bimaru*.

Delhi's Prof Ashish Bose, the man behind the concept and coinage of the BIMARU acronym, had carefully studied various parameters of a state's progress. He used the term to describe that most of north India's highly populous and large states like Bihar, Madhya Pradesh, Rajasthan and Uttar Pradesh were laggards on various development indices compared to their southern counterparts such as Kerala or Tamil Nadu.

The famed demographer, who was associated with the Jawaharlal Nehru University (JNU), Delhi, and had earlier headed the Population Research Centre at the Institute of Economic Growth, was working on a project with Prime Minister Rajiv Gandhi in the mid-eighties. It was when he was preparing the strategy paper on population and birth rates that he arranged the first letters of these four states to coin what became an important economic term, and then an unofficial guideline in official discussions and policy making for over 25 years in India. So in the acronym, BI stood for Bihar; MA for Madhya Pradesh; R for Rajasthan and U for Uttar Pradesh. BIMARU—since then has become a famous six-letter cuss word that forms the core of most development debates.

In his memoir *'Head Count'*, Prof Bose writes: "In my opinion these four states were demographically sick. Indicators covering the average age at marriage, the number of children per woman, the practice of family planning, the maternal and infant mortality rates, life expectancy at birth etc were the most dismal in these states."

Prof Bose further said: "After I presented my report to Rajiv Gandhi, he consulted his economic advisors who saw the logic of focussing attention only on four states, the 'BIMARU' states."

This background is vital to understand why the undivided and overpopulated states like MP, Bihar and UP were always looked down upon by policy makers from time to time. They required to put in more efforts, seek more central funding and thus organisations like the Planning Commission turned their binoculars towards these four states. Obviously, the BIMARU states were challenged states in more ways than one. When Prof Bose coined BIMARU, the Indian economy had not been thrown open to the world.

Nandan Nilekani, the co-founder of Infosys and head of the UPA's ambitious Aadhaar project, in his book *Imagining India— Ideas For The New Century* (2008), refers extensively to Madhya Pradesh's backwardness and quotes various scholars and researchers. Coming as it did from an acclaimed businessman and an ex-IITian, who made his well-researched observations 15-17 years after the Indian economy had been truly globalised, he enlarged the concept, meaning and scope of BIMARU and took it out of mere population related issues which were dominant in the '80s. Nilekani went on to add: "Education in other Indian states, however, had a very different trajectory. Today, only six states of India account for two-thirds of its children out of school—Andhra Pradesh, Bihar, Madhya Pradesh, Rajasthan, UP and West Bengal. The problems that have plagued these states stem in large part from their histories. Regions such as the BIMARU states had severe social problems, and they tended to infect state education schemes with them."

He also tried to impress upon us stating, "Caste tensions in

126 *Shivraj Singh And Rise Of Madhya Pradesh*

these states seeped into the schools, especially in the villages, where the schools are divided between the backward and upper castes."

Madhya Pradesh, the country's second largest state with close to 10% of land area (largest forest area at 94,689 sq km in the country) like many other Indian states, is home to a large number of castes and sub-castes. According to the state's Social Welfare Department, there are at least 48 scheduled primitive castes and 46 scheduled tribe primitive castes and as many as 91 other backward class (OBC) castes, not to speak of upper castes and people belonging to different religions and faiths. The studies of castes, tribes and sub-castes are quite intriguing, considering the ST population of 21% which is significantly higher than that of the country's which stands at 9% (MP Govt Memorandum to 14th Finance Commission/Feb 14).

A senior official in the Social Welfare Department explained in brief the complex caste scenario like this: "In the Gond tribe, there are many other names or sub-castes such as Ahuru, Asur, Arakh, Bada Maria, Bhima and Bhatola, to name just a few. Some castes like Meena are confined only to one sub-division of Sironj in Vidisha district of the state. There is a separate caste named as Bhil/Meena while Keer caste is found only in Bhopal, Raisen and Sehore districts."

Clearly, the demographic distribution is quite varied in the state. So bringing all of them into the mainstream, addressing their separate aspirations, solving issues like health and education or honouring their different customs and festivals besides adroitly looking at them as a 'vote bank' to provide benefits was indeed a Herculean task for a leader like Shivraj who had inherited a sufficiently backward region. The demands from these communities were very high. Digvijay Singh did try, in 2001, to address the 'Dalits' in a novel way but that did not help him at the hustings. But Shivraj started organising 'panchayats' to do his social engineering with a personal touch. The Chief Minister's Principal Secretary and once his college mate at Hamidia College in Bhopal, Manoj Shrivastava calls it 'social cementing' in the backdrop of the Dalit Agenda.

Why Shivraj stands tall among a host of chief ministers is due to his reasonable success in providing both social and physical infrastructure at the same time to people and almost turning around Madhya Pradesh from a backward state to one which topped the country in agriculture growth. It is not that others had not attempted this before but perhaps not so seriously and therefore not successfully, compared to say a Maharashtra or a Punjab or a Kerala of the '80s and '90s.

Towards the end of his first term, the Digvijay government's unique education schemes (EGS) had started making waves in the country. Several laudatory editorials and special articles by scholarly commentators had appeared in the English language newspapers then. For example, *The Economic Times* (Mumbai) on 26 August 1997, wrote an edit piece *'Ending BIMARU'* and took cognizance of Digvijay Singh's claims saying: "Mr Digvijay Singh claims that to tackle widespread goitre, his government decided not to expand subsidies but instead launch a campaign to educate tribals on the benefits of iodised salt. The result, he claims, is that the sale has improved... he also claims public education has helped reduce mortality from diarrhoea." In the end, the editorial sums up hoping, "If these claims hold up MP will cease to be a BIMARU state within a decade." In the next year's Assembly elections, the Congress came back (1998) and continued till 2003 but MP remained BIMARU, as various statistics suggested.

In 2001, the Digvijay government also formulated an ambitious economic development policy which saw formation—for the first time—of MP Economic Development Board (MPEDB). In his introduction to the 190-page policy document Digvijay Singh had

128 *Shivraj Singh And Rise Of Madhya Pradesh*

written: "The overarching theme of our development strategy is connectivity... connectivity not only in a physical sense but more importantly of connecting people... the state has put people at the centre of its development strategy...." Unfortunately for Digvijay Singh, people of Madhya Pradesh did not believe in his government or his words. Within two years of introduction of the policy (and eight years in power continuously) that was supposed to be connecting with people and providing overall economic development to them, his government was ousted from power by the BJP which won by a huge majority.

The lofty idea of forming a board like that did not translate into reality the way it was envisioned. Top industries were not attracted to MP nor was there agriculture growth, as witnessed in the corresponding eight years under Shivraj Singh.

About hunger, food insecurity and poor health facilities in MP, negative comments and figures were routinely appearing in the media and various research findings. The 2008 India State Hunger Index and the Global Hunger Index of the same year had equated MP with Ethiopia with 30.87% as the score, against that of India which stood at 23.3% which was the country's overall hunger index. Bihar was equated with Yemen at 27.30% and Punjab had fared well with 13.63% which equalled the Philippines. MP was considered an extremely alarming state. The 2008 Global Hunger Report made use of the 1999 statistics—the era of Congress in MP.

According to a story in *Hindustan Times,* Delhi, by Kounteya Sinha in 2011, the infant mortality rate (IMR) of MP was 59, compared to Manipur where it was 11. In other words, out of 1,000 babies born, 59 died in MP against 11 in Manipur; in Odisha and UP the figure stood at 57 in the corresponding period. Another recent story of the same paper says 62 of the 331 critically ill newborns

*Banishing the BIMARU* 129

died in five months at the Harda district's Sick New-born Care Unit (SNCU). Deplorably, the unit was set up in August 2013, according to the paper report which quoted the CMHO, Dr J Avasya.

But Chief Minister Chouhan told me he had taken adequate measures and things were surely improving. He pointed to the state's health budget that had gone up manifold over the years. If MP's health budget in 2008-09 was ₹ 1,389 crore, by 2013-14 it zoomed to ₹ 4,147 crore—a three-fold rise. This also includes what is called the fiscal transfers, that is, the Union Government's contribution to states under various schemes either through the Finance Commission or through the Planning Commission. In the state's health sector, 1/3rd of the total budget share comes from Delhi and major portion comes under the National Rural Health Mission (NHRM). Some of these transfers are conditional and some unconditional and there is a running debate over the issue. However, as noted earlier, the crucial IMR dropped in MP to 56 in 2012 which in 2009 stood at 67—the highest in India then, with UP coming close at 63 and Bihar at 52. (Source: SRS 2013. Indian average was at 42 for IMR and 178 for MMR.)

What did MP do to bring down the IMR? What was the strategy, if any? Health department officials say institutional deliveries which were somewhere around 40% or so showed a quantum jump to 80-90%. The Ministry of Health and Family Welfare GoI had launched a unique cash assistance programme—Janani Suraksha Yojana (JSY) in April 2005. Various population-based surveys, such as International Institute of Population Studies, show that the JSY did make a difference and as a result institutional deliveries grew manifold. MP too was a beneficiary of the scheme. A former principal secretary (health) believes that overall awareness, coupled with education among women and girls, also helped in IMR going

# 130 Shivraj Singh And Rise Of Madhya Pradesh

down in a society where economic growth had become quite evident. Timely immunization and nutrition through *anganwadis* (whatever may have been the quality of food as the supply chain of raw materials and cooked food has been in the hands of unscrupulous private contractors whose unholy nexus with politicians and officials has been too well known in MP) changed the condition.

Table 1:

Growth of State GSDP in the last three years

| State | 2011-12 | 2012-13 | 2013-14 | Average* |
|---|---|---|---|---|
| AP/Telangana | 7.51 | 5.09 | 5.51 | 6.04 |
| Assam | 5.33 | 6.06 | 5.87 | 5.75 |
| Bihar | 9.58 | 15.05 | 8.82 | 11.15 |
| Chhattisgarh | 1.49 | 7.56 | 7.05 | 5.37 |
| Gujarat | 7.66 | 7.96 | NA | 7.81 |
| Haryana | 7.79 | 6.52 | – | 7.08 |
| Himachal Pradesh | 7.31 | 6.14 | 6.24 | 6.56 |
| Jammu & Kashmir | 6.20 | 5.50 | 5.88 | 5.86 |
| Jharkhand | 9.39 | 7.87 | 8.33 | 8.53 |
| Kerala | 7.96 | 8.24 | NA | 8.10 |
| Madhya Pradesh | 9.69 | 9.89 | 11.08 | 10.12 |
| Maharashtra | 7.10 | 7.13 | NA | 7.12 |
| Odisha | 3.78 | 8.09 | 5.60 | 5.82 |
| Rajasthan | 5.17 | 4.52 | 4.60 | 4.76 |
| Tamil Nadu | 7.42 | 4.14 | 6.13 | 5.90 |
| Uttar Pradesh | 6.45 | 5.51 | 5.20 | 5.72 |
| Uttarakhand | 9.35 | 9.01 | 9.99 | 9.45 |
| All-India GDP** | 6.69 | 4.47 | 4.85 | 5.34 |

*3 year average, **(2004-05 base)

Source: Central Statistics Office (CSO) Planning Commission; Courtesy: Indian Express

*Banishing the BIMARU* 131

If the social sector was focussed upon in this manner with numerous policy interventions, industrial infrastructure and facilities too were targeted through the biennial global industry summits in Khajuraho and Indore where top industrialists signed MoUs on the spot and expressed their intent to be partners in progress with the MP government. Anil Ambani of the Reliance Group has been repeatedly visiting MP. His ₹ 25,000 crore coal-based power project at Sasan in Singrauli district has already been commissioned (1320 Mw) and investment of over ₹ 17,000 crore is seen on the ground, a company spokesman told me. Arun Bhatt, IAS and MD, MP Industrial Development Corporation (MPSIDC), supports the claim. His other project is Reliance Cement which brought another ₹ 2,500 crore investment. Both projects are operational since 2013. The 2012 Global Industry Summit (28-30 October) at Indore was marked by the presence of Shashi Ruia of the Essar Group, Subrata Roy, Chairman of Sahara Group, Kumar Mangalam Birla of Aditya Birla Group, Abhay Firodia of Force Motors and Adi Godrej of the country's well-known Godrej group, among many others. The Leader of Opposition in the Lok Sabha, Sushma Swaraj, and BJP stalwart LK Advani had participated in the meet to make it a successful venture. MoUs close to rupees one lakh crore (*Indian Express*, dated 30 October 2012) were signed in two days in different sectors from heavy industries to horticulture. Ambani made a significant statement that MP would soon become the country's power capital. "Shivraj is a visionary like my father (Dhirubhai)", Anil Ambani said at the Global Investor Summit, Indore on 29 October 2012.

The MP industry summits may not have been as high profile or result-oriented events as Narendra Modi's Vibrant Gujarat (In 2013 Japan and Canada were partners with Gujarat government and close

132 *Shivraj Singh And Rise Of Madhya Pradesh*

to 100 Japanese companies participated in it.) but they were no less earnest. They created an industry-friendly climate in the state which was missing earlier. According to Bhatt, in 2014 Volvo-Eicher will set up their 7th plant in MP near Bhopal.

Normally seen in a simple *kurta-pyjama,* Shivraj was looking confident in Indore in a *Jodhpuri bandh gala* (traditional ceremonial high neck attire) welcoming the top industry honchos with consummate ease. He was an instant hero among the industry captains of the country.

Power generation and distribution scenario too improved year after year to make MP a power-surplus state under the Shivraj regime. Bureaucrats in the energy department tell me that management of the surplus power itself is a headache now. If in 2003, power generation was 4,673 Mw, in 2013, it grew to 10,600 Mw. According to Government sources industrial investment at present is pegged at ₹ 85,000 crore which was a paltry ₹ 7,935 crore in 2003, the year BJP came to power and Digvijay had slipped into history, if not into oblivion.

There was a time when industry captains would shudder to think of MP, not to talk of considering the state among their first choice to set up plants. Things have changed a lot now though much more is still required to be done. As an ASSOCHAM report of September 2010 comments: "The challenge before the state is to attract investment in industry... it has to take proactive measures so that investment flows on the basis of the attractiveness of a destination in terms of quality infrastructure, skilled human resource, policy environment and good governance."

No surprise then that the BJP had made *sushasan* (good governance) as one of its major election planks. Not only did advertisements showing Atal Bihari Vajpayee's smiling face telling

*Banishing the BIMARU*    133

people about '*sushasan*' appear in newspapers but work was also being done on the field for attracting investments in record time. A year before the 2013 elections, two Indian MNCs—Infosys Technologies Ltd and Tata Consultancy Services—were allotted sprawling land of 100 acres each near the Devi Ahilyabai Holkar Airport in Indore, the growing IT hub of the state with top-class air connectivity for setting up their two separate SEZs. According to Akash Tripathi, District Collector, Indore, the land was acquired by the Indore Development Authority (IDA) and handed over to the Information Technology Department which in turn gave it to the IT majors—all within the space of about 15 months. NR Narayana Murthy, the founder Chairman of Infosys, laid the foundation stone on 24 February 2014, heralding a new era in industrialisation in Madhya Pradesh. The state's IT Department Secretary, Hari Ranjan Rao, IAS, says the government finalised the land lease deeds with the IT companies in October 2012. These legal documents protect the interests of the government as well as the investors. "We had to go to the Cabinet a number of times to get things cleared but government responded very quickly which has impressed the blue chip IT companies who got land for ₹ 20 lakh per acre," Rao clarified.

No industrialist likes delays and red tape as it affects their deadlines and targets. Therefore, industrialists prefer to go to states which respond with sensitivity and speed. If MP lagged behind in industry, one of the prime reasons was the indifference of politicians and bureaucracy in the past.

**Table 2: State GDP growth (%) at constant (2004-05) prices.**

| States/UTs | 2005-06 | 2006-07 | 2007-08 | 2008-09 | 2009-10 | 2010-11 | 2011-12 | Average |
|---|---|---|---|---|---|---|---|---|
| Andhra Pradesh | 9.57 | 11.18 | 12.02 | 6.81 | 4.53 | 9.66 | 7.82 | 8.81 |
| Arunachal Pradesh | 2.75 | 5.25 | 12.06 | 8.73 | 9.86 | 1.25 | 10.84 | 7.25 |
| Assam | 3.4 | 4.65 | 4.82 | 5.72 | 9.00 | 7.89 | 6.47 | 5.99 |
| Bihar | 0.17 | 15.69 | 5.72 | 12.16 | 7.09 | 11.29 | 13.26 | 9.34 |
| Chhattisgarh | 3.23 | 18.6 | 8.61 | 8.39 | 3.42 | 9.75 | 8.14 | 8.59 |
| Goa | 7.54 | 10.02 | 5.54 | 10.02 | 10.20 | 10.15 | 9.39 | 8.98 |
| Gujarat | 14.95 | 8.39 | 11.00 | 6.78 | 11.25 | 10.00 | 8.53 | 10.13 |
| Haryana | 9.20 | 11.22 | 8.45 | 8.17 | 11.72 | 8.84 | 7.92 | 9.36 |
| Himachal Pradesh | 8.43 | 9.09 | 8.55 | 7.42 | 8.09 | 8.74 | 7.44 | 8.25 |
| Jammu and Kashmir | 5.78 | 5.95 | 6.40 | 6.46 | 4.51 | 5.96 | 6.22 | 5.90 |
| Jharkhand | -3.20 | 2.38 | 20.52 | -1.75 | 10.14 | 8.67 | 8.92 | 6.53 |
| Karnataka | 10.51 | 9.98 | 12.60 | 7.11 | 1.29 | 9.66 | 5.50 | 8.09 |
| Kerala | 10.09 | 7.90 | 8.77 | 5.56 | 9.17 | 8.05 | 9.51 | 8.44 |
| Madhya Pradesh | 5.31 | 9.23 | 4.69 | 12.47 | 9.88 | 7.13 | 11.81 | 8.65 |
| Maharashtra | 13.35 | 13.53 | 11.26 | 2.58 | 9.17 | 11.34 | 8.54 | 9.97 |
| Manipur | 6.35 | 2.00 | 5.96 | 6.56 | 6.89 | 5.07 | 6.71 | 5.65 |

Continued...

*Banishing the BIMARU* 135

| States/UTs | 2005-05 | 2006-07 | 2007-08 | 2008-09 | 2009-10 | 2010-11 | 2011-12 | Average |
|---|---|---|---|---|---|---|---|---|
| Meghalaya | 7.91 | 7.74 | 4.51 | 12.94 | 6.55 | 8.72 | 6.31 | 7.81 |
| Mizoram | 6.97 | 4.78 | 10.98 | 13.34 | 12.38 | 7.25 | 10.09 | 9.40 |
| Nagaland | 10.22 | 7.80 | 7.31 | 6.34 | 6.90 | 5.46 | 5.09 | 7.02 |
| Orissa | 5.68 | 12.85 | 10.94 | 7.75 | 4.55 | 7.50 | 4.92 | 7.74 |
| Punjab | 5.90 | 10.18 | 9.05 | 5.85 | 6.29 | 6.53 | 5.94 | 7.11 |
| Rajasthan | 6.68 | 11.67 | 5.14 | 9.09 | 6.70 | 15.28 | 6.11 | 8.67 |
| Sikkim | 9.78 | 6.02 | 7.61 | 16.39 | 73.61 | 8.13 | 8.17 | 18.53 |
| Tamil Nadu | 13.96 | 15.21 | 6.13 | 4.89 | 10.36 | 9.83 | 7.37 | 9.68 |
| Tripura | 5.82 | 8.28 | 7.70 | 9.44 | 10.65 | 8.20 | 8.67 | 8.39 |
| Uttar Pradesh | 6.51 | 8.07 | 7.32 | 6.99 | 6.58 | 7.81 | 6.86 | 7.16 |
| Uttarakhand | 14.34 | 13.59 | 18.12 | 12.65 | 18.13 | 9.94 | 5.28 | 13.15 |
| West Bengal | 6.29 | 7.79 | 7.76 | 4.90 | 8.03 | 9.22 | 6.58 | 7.22 |
| Andaman and Nicobar Island | 5.18 | 18.04 | 10.13 | 14.32 | 13.20 | 8.20 | 6.14 | 10.74 |
| Chandigarh | 10.69 | 14.68 | 7.28 | 8.10 | 9.96 | 8.23 | 7.11 | 9.44 |
| Delhi | 10.05 | 12.39 | 11.19 | 12.92 | 10.94 | 10.92 | 11.34 | 11.39 |
| Puducherry | 24.92 | 3.69 | 8.59 | 8.66 | 15.72 | 10.6 | 2.40 | 10.58 |
| All India GDP (2004-05 base) | 9.48 | 9.57 | 9.32 | 6.72 | 8.59 | 9.32 | 6.21 | 8.46 |

Source: Website Central Statistical Organisation; Few selected UTs have been included.

## 136 *Shivraj Singh And Rise Of Madhya Pradesh*

With the contribution of the industry sector to the Gross State Domestic Product (GSDP) at current prices at a base year of 2004-05, MP showed a growth of about 3% from 10.12% in 2005-06, to a significant jump of 13.00% in 2012-13, according to the Centre for Monitoring Indian Economy (CMIE), an independent body. Other leading states like Maharashtra (13%), TN (13%), UP (11%), Karnataka (8%) and AP (6%) performed well to be considered among the 'top five' in the country in the corresponding year.

## Digvijay Singh's Efforts

At this stage, let me explain in brief why I have delved so much into the BIMARU aspect of MP and related factors. While Shivraj Singh is on record saying (before the Planning Commission on several occasions) that MP is no longer a BIMARU state, there was an ex-chief minister who had actually gone out of his way in the interest of MP to meet Prof Bose in Delhi, pleading with him to "take the BIMARU tag off Madhya Pradesh," which Bose had steadfastly refused to do. BIMARU was such a socio-political stigma that it had prevented industrial investments into the affected states. It also held back the state from being ranked anywhere higher among competing states in a globalised economy.

Both, Prof Bose and a former BBC correspondent in India, Daniel Lak, a Canadian, had shared this incident about Digvijay Singh personally with me in Bhopal a few years ago.

What Lak has written in his book, *Mantras of Change—Reporting India In A Time of Flux*, is worth a read for it throws enough light on the disadvantages of being labelled a backward state. According to Lak: "From the last census in 1991, both Rajasthan and Madhya Pradesh have shown some upward trends in economic growth and literacy. But not nearly upward enough for Bose to redefine or come

Banishing the BIMARU 137

up with a new acronym." Lak added, "A while ago the Chief Minister of Madhya Pradesh went to Bose and said, 'see things are getting better, now take us out of BIMARU'." Bose said, "No way can your state be considered progressive yet. You have still got shockingly low female literacy, high infant mortality and other problems... your statistical improvements are largely among men and urban dwellers... keep working on it."

Lak then adds on his own: "Being categorised by Bose as Chief Minister of a backward state may not lose you any votes but the man that Bose was referring to, Digvijay Singh of the Congress Party, was defeated in state elections in November 2003, largely because of voter dissatisfaction with his government's record on development."

It was Digvijay Singh who had, in late '90s, made a surprising statement, "...elections are not won by development works but are won by management,"during a press conference in the state-owned Hotel Palash. To support his argument he had cited the example of Lalu Prasad Yadav who, he said, had won an election in Bihar without doing much developmental work. Later, at an investors' summit at Khajuraho on 10 December 1999, where I was present, Digvijay Singh had surprised the gathering of industrialists and investors saying, "I know travelling on Madhya Pradesh roads is a nightmarish experience." In the same week, after his official meeting with Union Minister of State for Tourism, Uma Bharti, at Bhopal's Ashoka Lake View Hotel, when I had referred to his Khajuraho statement and sought to know why the roads were just not improving in the state and why he was not getting tough with the PWD engineers, he smilingly asked me: "*Kya dande mar kar kam karwaaun un logon se?* (Do I beat them to get work done ?)"

But one important thing happened after Khajuraho. MP Rajan, IAS, high-profile MD of MPSIDC, till then close to CM, was

## 138  *Shivraj Singh And Rise Of Madhya Pradesh*

removed from industry and dumped into the Mantralaya, where he had never worked before. There he came directly under the Chief Secretary. He preferred to put in his papers and took voluntary retirement. Digvijay by then, had perhaps realised the need for physical development and speedy development at that.

After bifurcation of the state 14 years ago, with more of the underdeveloped portion going away into Chhattisgarh, Madhya Pradesh's perception is still that of a BIMARU state, though concerted efforts in the past many years under the Shivraj's regime show multi-sectoral improvement, a fact being accepted at the national level now.

## Shivraj On BIMARU

When did Shivraj Singh hear the word BIMARU and its connotation—political and social? What did he do to get out of that defamatory club?

He told me that he had heard of BIMARU many years ago when he was in Delhi as an MP. "Madhya Pradesh *ke bare me aisa sab sunkar ki ye fissaddi rajya hai, dil dukhta tha... kuchh thos karne ki ichha usi samay se man mein thi* (It used to hurt, hearing repeatedly about MP as a laggard state, and there has been a burning desire in me to change all that since then).

But, according to him, MP is no longer a BIMARU state, nor is anyone in a responsible position in the Union Government now talking about it being so. He shared this with me in February 2014, soon after meeting the Prime Minister Dr Manmohan Singh and Finance Minister P Chidambaram in Delhi on issues related to the support price of *chana* (gram).

The Planning Commission Deputy Chairman, Montek Singh Ahluwalia, in a recently published article, *Ensuring Regional Balance in Indian Planning*, writes about MP's growth while reasoning the planning process and the economic disparities, with specific focus on the BIMARU states. Prof Bose had, a few years down the line, added O (for Odisha) and now the acronym is slightly amended as BIMAROU, while retaining the same pronunciation and meaning.

It is in this Odisha state that Korput-Bolangir-Kalahandi, popularly known as KBK districts, had shot into limelight in the '70s through the '90s as the poorest and most backward districts of the country.

Ahluwalia further adds: "The concern that economic disparities across states may be widening was explicitly noted in the Mid-Term Appraisal of the Ninth Plan (1997-2001) published in 2000. The Tenth Five Year Plan (2002-2007), for the first time, set state-specific targets for growth and poverty reduction in individual states, and this practice continued in both Eleventh and also the Twelfth Plan. The establishment of state-specific targets, endorsed by the states, means that performance against these targets can now be monitored, and the implications for the changes in regional balance, they entail, can be measured."

Taking stock of states' imbalance up to the Tenth Plan, Ahluwalia says their performance has improved substantially in the recent years. "Madhya Pradesh, the second state in the BIMAROU grouping, performed better than Bihar in earlier years, and it too has since improved over time. From a growth rate of 6.6% for undivided Madhya Pradesh in the Eighth Plan period, the two states of Madhya Pradesh and Chhattisgarh grew at 9.2% and 7.7% respectively, in the Eleventh Plan period."

In his essay, the Planning Commission deputy chief at one place states: "It is useful to consider what the Twelfth Plan targets for growth in the poorer state imply for convergence. Madhya Pradesh

## 140 *Shivraj Singh And Rise Of Madhya Pradesh*

at 8.8% (and Jharkhand at 8.5%) are targeting faster growth than the 8.0% national target, but since the growth of population in these states is significantly higher than for the country as a whole, the growth rates of per capita income in these states are not likely to be higher than the national average...."

What a confident Shivraj Singh claimed in New Delhi at the BJP national executive committee meeting in mid-January 2014, a month after winning the Assembly polls, is also recognised by noted economist Sawaminathan S Anklesaria Aiyar, though separately. Shivraj had stated: "If a nation's growth is maintained at 4 or 5%, it is due to BJP - ruled states only." Incidentally, Madhya Pradesh has registered a double-digit growth consistently in the past seven years and this year, according to Planning Commission, Delhi's figures, (released in March 2014) MP has topped in GSDP growth in the country which actually takes away the BIMARU tag.

Aiyar, writing on, *Lessons in Development From the Bimaru States*, (*The New Bihar—Rekindling Governance and Development*, Ed: NK Singh and Nicholas Stern-2013), says: ...emergence of new breed of chief ministers, all non-Congress politicians, who after 2000 set about transforming states once regarded as irremediably backward, the remarkable outcome is that many of these (BIMARU) states have now started growing faster than the national average (Table 2). Instead of pulling India down, they are now pulling India up." Aiyar opines that the new breed of chief ministers generated very rapid GDP growth with new policies rather than just new investments. Shivraj did exactly that; he made user-friendly policies and investments followed gradually.

How did the MP Chief Minister Shivraj Singh bring about a Green Revolution? How did he lay special emphasis on power generation and build other infrastructure that led to the state's overall growth has been mentioned earlier in the relevant chapters. His visit to Delhi for one and a half hours in the second week of February 2014 to have brief meetings with the PM and the FM on the farmers' welfare issue stands testimony to his concern for farmers. In my relatively long journalistic career, having seen the working of close to 10 Chief Ministers, I can impartially say that not many of his predecessors took so much personal pain for the growth of farmers and for Madhya Pradesh.

The credible figures of the State Government and the GoI, besides comments of experts like Aiyar and specific observations of the Planning Commission about rapid growth of MP, are reasons enough for Shivraj Singh not needing to knock at the doors of Ashish Bose in Delhi.

രുരുരു

## Chapter - 11

# DARKNESS AT NOON

Any meaningful discourse on contemporary politics in Madhya Pradesh shall remain incomplete without a detailed mention of Digvijay Singh, his art of administration and the 10-year rule of the Congress Party under his leadership from 1993-2003. It had its highs and lows in politics and administration and consequent impact on the society.

His performance (or lack of it) harmed Digvijay Singh a great deal politically. As a penance he went into self-proclaimed political exile for 10 years saying he would not take up any post or fight elections. At the end of the 10 years, his party nominated him to the Rajya Sabha and he readily agreed, but before that he was an all-powerful AICC general secretary. So his political exile did not really mean much to his detractors.

Following the Babri Masjid's demolition on 6 December 1992, the three BJP-ruled state governments dismissed by PV Narasimha Rao-led Congress government included the Sunderlal Patwa regime in MP. Patwa was in power for close to three years (5 March 1990-15 December 1992). This was his second short stint in power, the earlier one was after the end of the Emergency in 1977 when the newly-formed coalition of the Janata Party came to power, of

## 144 Shivraj Singh And Rise Of Madhya Pradesh

which the Jan Sangh was the dominant constituent. None of the three chief ministers between June 1977 and February 1980 could last their full term. The first was Kailash Joshi, the second Virendra Kumar Saklecha and the last was Patwa, who demitted office on 17 February 1980.

Later, the Morarji Desai led Janata Party government collapsed at the Centre due to internal bickering and the party split over the dual membership issue with the socialist group refusing to work with RSS members (Vajpayee, Advani, Sikander Baktha) and walking away. However, Congress propped it up by giving support to Chaudhary Charan Singh (Bhartiya Lok Dal) who became the PM but that government also proved to be short-lived. Jan Sangh, one of the largest constituents of the coalition, refused to disown its RSS links and the motley coalition, cobbled together by common hatred for Indira Gandhi, fell apart, saddening Jayaprakash Narayan. Jan Sangh then emerged in its new *avatar* as the Bhartiya Janata Party (BJP) on 6 April, 1980 at Delhi's Ferozeshah Kotla ground .

After the Centre dismissed the Patwa government in 1992 the state remained under President's Rule till the latter part of 1993. Digvijay Singh was then the Pradesh Congress Party president and an MP. When Assembly elections took place in November, the Congress returned to power with a thumping majority and much of the credit was legitimately given to Digvijay Singh, who had as the organisation head toiled hard to install his party in power.

So when the Congress trounced the BJP, returning 174 MLAs in a House of 320 seats in the undivided Madhya Pradesh, Digvijay was the natural front-runner for the top job though he was not among the legislators. He was a sitting MP from Rajgarh, a Lok Sabha seat in the backward district close to capital Bhopal. Singh comes from a family of Thakurs from Raghogarh, part of the old Gwalior state where he is popularly called *'Raja saab'* while elsewhere he is known as Diggi Raja.

The election of the Congress Legislature Party (CLP) became a memorable chapter in the political history of Madhya Pradesh for all its drama, deceit and intrigue. Shyama Charan Shukla, three-time Chief Minister of the State between 1969 and 1990, had thrown his hat once again in the ring. He was the youngest CM when he first came to power in 1969. Perhaps he was confident that Narasimha Rao (then AICC president and Prime Minister and also close to his family) would cast his weight behind him. After the Tirupati and Surajkund AICC sessions, Rao's open dislike for dissident Arjun Singh, the real villain in the CLP election in his home state, was sufficient to kindle Shukla's hopes. Shukla had once told me over his specially brewed aromatic tea and *namkeen* (he was a generous and a warm host) at his Shyamla Hills residence in Bhopal, that "Rao had completed his college studies while staying at his father Ravi Shankar Shukla's home in Nagpur." Rao and Shukla had been family friends for decades and contemporaries in politics, though from different states, Rao being four years senior to Shukla and the more seasoned and astute politician of the two.

In the hot race for the MP Chief Minister's office, the other heavyweights were Kamal Nath, Madhavrao Scindia and Subhash Yadav. In the CLP meeting, Arjun Singh pressed for Yadav's name. Yadav being a backward would have proved to be a stumbling block for the 'towering' Brahmin, SC Shukla, Singh's arch-rival, to stop him from becoming the CM yet again. This led to a triangular fight—or so it seemed—between Digvijay Singh, Shukla and Yadav. But Yadav's name did not win favour with a large number of newly-elected MLAs despite Arjun Singh's backing. Vir Sanghvi, a close friend of Madhavrao Scindia and former Editor of *Hindustan Times,*

146 *Shivraj Singh And Rise Of Madhya Pradesh*

in his book, *Madhavrao Scindia: A Life*, claimed: "Arjun Singh and Madhavrao had put aside their own personal differences to rout BJP... and Madhavrao had no objection to Yadav's name. He, however, was opposed to Digvijay Singh, an old Arjun Singh protégé. Incidentally, in MP politics the 'backward card' and the 'tribal card' have been used by upper caste (Congress) politicians brazenly from time to time but they never allowed any of the backward or tribals to reach the top post. Shiv Bhanu Singh Solanki, a tribal leader from Dhar had won the Congress Legislature Party (CLP) election to be the CM in 1980 but Arjun Singh dramatically became the CM, with Sanjay Gandhi's last-minute blessings. The other tribal leader was Jamuna Devi and backward leader was Subhash Yadav who could never make the Shyamla Hills mansion their home and had to contend with Dy Chief Ministership. Solanki too was made the number two to Arjun Singh. In BJP, caste plays an important role but not as important as in the Congress party. OBC leaders Uma Bharti and Shivraj both are recent examples of those who could easily become the CM.

So, a night before the CLP meet, 90 odd MLAs owing allegiance to the wily Thakur from Sidhi (Churhat), declared their support for Digvijay, taking everyone by surprise. If it had happened with tacit understanding between the two Thakurs, it never came to light. In the meeting, Arjun Singh kept shouting about a backward caste candidate; gave a highly emotional speech in favour of the backward without letting anyone get the slightest hint of his changed game plan. After his speech, he slowly walked out of the assembly of MLAs, shocking everyone, including the central observers. Clearly, Subhash Yadav was left high and dry. Singh's 'support' to a backward leader had evaporated within a day's time. Yadav could not understand

*Darkness at Noon* 147

the high-level caste politics… much later he was made Dy Chief Minister.

For want of a clear consensus, the observers Pranab Mukherjee and Sushil Shinde, held a secret ballot in which Digvijay won. It was apparently reduced to a straight fight between traditional political rivals in MP—Thakurs and Brahmins. There was no formal election held but Digvijay clearly had the backing of 70% MLAs and was an obvious choice, having been a decisive force in the distribution of party tickets just about a month ago. SC Shukla, a narcissist, was out of touch with ground reality and thus lost his chance to wear the crown for the fourth time.

Sanghvi, quoting Amar Singh, who was then one of Scindia's advisers, says, "Arjun Singh and Madhavrao Scindia had reached an understanding that Scindia will go to MP leaving Arjun Singh free to take another shot at Delhi." Sanghvi further says quoting Amar Singh, "I (Amar) knew Arjun Singh could not be trusted and so I advised Madhavrao *ji* to remain in Delhi until he had heard from him."

Eventually, a sullen Scindia remained stranded in Delhi; backward Yadav was left fuming and fretting; Shukla kept wondering what had happened to his supporters overnight, as Digvijay Singh came out with flying colours to be the popular CM of a vast state.

## The Digvijay Story

Digvijay Singh's highly absorbing and long political story laced with successes and failures, actually began from here (December 1993) when he was sworn in as the young, charming CM of a huge state. And the story goes on till the last week of January 2014, when he sprang yet another political surprise and pocketed the lone Rajya

148 *Shivraj Singh And Rise Of Madhya Pradesh*

Sabha seat unanimously for at least six years. His nomination came at a time when he was at the receiving end of all-round criticism from within his own party for the poor showing against Shivraj Singh's BJP. *Dainik Bhaskar,* Bhopal, reported on 29 January 2014 that Sajjan Singh Verma, an MP from Dewas reserved constituency and a former minister under Digvijay, had launched a blistering attack on the Congress high command for nominating Singh to the Upper House of Parliament, saying, "Singh was instrumental in the humiliating defeat of the party and was yet nominated for the coveted seat." Sajjan Singh is considered as a Kamal Nath acolyte in state politics. People close to Digvijay however maintain that he did not seek the RS nomination on his own but just a day before the filing of papers, the Congress president Sonia Gandhi personally asked him to file the papers in Bhopal. She apparently wanted a 'trusted' man free for advice and help during the most crucial Lok Sabha elections for the Congress, in April-May 2014.

In his own words, "I will never in my life ever ditch the Gandhi family. Whatever I am today, I am because of this family. Even when Mr Narasimha Rao was the Prime Minister, when Soniaji and he were not getting on too well, against all indications I went to Amethi. I will never, never, never in my life ditch this family." He had stated this in an interview with ND Sharma, Correspondent of *Indian Express*, soon after winning his first term, in 1998.

There were stories doing the rounds that Digvijay was looking for a safe Lok Sabha seat to fight and names other than Rajgarh were in circulation. Sagar constituency was also one of them. Clearly he wanted to end his exile with a resounding return to 'active politics'. But he developed cold feet after the party's defeat in Assembly polls as his winning chances appeared suspect. A former PCC spokesman quipped: "If such a senior leader is not confident of his victory and

*Darkness at Noon*  149

prefers the Rajya Sabha route to Parliament, how can others be motivated to contest elections in such tough times?"

Digvijay Singh's decade-long rule over Madhya Pradesh, the first of its kind by any party till then, stood testimony to umpteen politically significant events. Major happenings and controversies like De Beers diamond mining, land scams and industry scams such as the ₹ 719 crore Inter-Corporate Deposit (ICD) scam, setting up of Justice GG Sohoni Commission to trace the bureaucrat-politician-criminal nexus, Havala case of 1996 that outraged Arjun Singh, VC Shukla and Madhavrao Scindia; then the floating of breakaway political outfits by Arjun Singh (Tiwari Congress under ND Tiwari) and Scindia (MP Vikas Congress) and their merger back into the Congress, Arjun Singh's defeat in the Lok Sabha election from Hoshangabad, creation of unique 'district governments' to fast track decision-making, the Chief Minister's unique mass village contact programme, his open conflict with Governor Dr Bhai Mahavir—the well-read nationalist leader from RSS background.

Then there was also growing Naxalism, murder of a Cabinet Minister in tribal Balaghat district, release of first Human Development report (HDR) at the hands of Prof Amartya Sen in Delhi (Jan 99); introducing a progressive population policy that stipulated two-child norm (Jan 2000), completion of the imposing Vidhan Sabha building by Charles Correa and its vastu-related issues, first White Paper on the state's worsening financial health (February 1999), bifurcation of the state that gave birth to Chhattisgarh in November 2000, tricky allocation of cadres to IAS, IPS, IFS officers and other government officials, a ₹ 10 crore bribe charge against the CM to help a liquor baron from Bhopal (from which the Lokayukta absolved him in 2002) and his famous letter to PM Vajpayee (dated 28 August 2001) on the same issue as Digvijay's name was dragged into it. Finally, the faulty implementation of a highly controversial 'Dalit Agenda', which many believe proved to be the last straw on the camel's back.

Digvijay Singh suffered the most humiliating defeat in the state's history in 2003 due to the perceived high corruption, poor governance and general callousness towards people, lack of seriousness at the highest level as also the BSP—*Bijli-Sadak-Pani*—problems. However, the lion's share of the blame should go to the social rift his agenda caused among the Dalits and other castes. Though it was termed by him as 'charting a new course for Dalits for the 21$^{st}$ century', it ended up charting a course to nowhere, literally!

The Congress continues to be exiled from power since 2003, thanks to Digvijay brand of politics which proved to be a boon for the BJP.

It is not that he did just nothing. Having declared boldly, "Our disadvantage will be advantage," in an interview to *Businessline* (September 1995), he worked on the social sector but not on infrastructure. He decentralised powers under Panchayati Raj, started Rajiv Gandhi missions on education, watershed, food security and diarrhoea control and so on to help people. He launched Education Guarantee Schemes which were praised by the English media, even internationally. *The Los Angeles Times* wrote a story in December 1999 'Ending Centuries of Illiteracy' and observed: "A social revolution is sweeping India in the form of an education guarantee programme. Thousands of isolated villages are taking the government up on its offer of a teacher and books for the asking."

Digvijay's first term from 1993-1998 passed rather peacefully, though it was during this term he had conceded that, "my administration was lax (93-98)" and said, "he needed to be tough" (IE-Dec, 1998).

The second one ran into several hurdles and turned out to be quite eventful despite the fact that the state had shrunk and most of those who were at odds with the Raja like the Shukla brothers, tribal leader Arvind Netam, former CM Motilal Vora and his sworn enemy Ajit Jogi moved away to the new state and ceased to be political pinpricks and Digvijay could breathe easy. It was during this tenure that Digvijay appeared to many people a changed leader. In his first Cabinet meeting of the second term, on 8 December 1998, he devised a code of conduct for all ministers. The code expected the ministers' conduct and deeds to create a model of governance for the entire country. "The conduct of the ministers should not generate animosity or hatred in the society along caste or communal lines," it read. Ironically enough, his government brought in, towards the end of its term, a divisive programme in the name of helping the Dalits. The code got a quiet burial with many ministers facing serious charges of corruption. Rajendra Singh, a close relative of Arjun Singh and an accused in the industries scam of ICD, secured bail in Bhopal in January-February 2014 after he was elected Deputy Speaker of the new Assembly. He was an important minister in Digvijay Singh's Cabinet. The ICD scandal of late '90s lingers on as the two industrialist brothers, once close to Digvijay Singh, were sentenced to imprisonment by a special court around the same time, in Indore.

## The Raipur Episode

After recalling a shocking incident related to Digvijay Singh, I will relate details of the otherwise noble cause of Dalit upliftment that recoiled on him.

Digvijay learned the hard way how politics compels one to do what one abhors. Ajit Jogi had to be made chief minister of the

## 152 *Shivraj Singh And Rise Of Madhya Pradesh*

designated new state by Digvijay Singh, 'under instructions from the top', despite his complete reluctance to support him. When Digvijay was a minister in Arjun Singh's Cabinet, Jogi was serving as district collector of Indore. In 1986, Arjun Singh made him quit the IAS and got him nominated to the Rajya Sabha. But no love was lost between Digvijay Singh and Jogi although both were from the Arjun Singh camp. When the small state of Chhattisgarh was carved out of Madhya Pradesh without much demand or agitation, Sonia Gandhi directed Digvijay Singh to ensure that Jogi became the CM and not VC Shukla.

As chief of the *Hindustan Times* Bureau, at Bhopal, I was in Raipur to witness the birth of the new state where the multi-layered drama unfolded. Digvijay had admitted before a select group of journalists the evening before the CLP meeting that he was just obeying the party's orders of making the former bureaucrat the first CM of the new state... against his own wishes. He kept meeting for the whole day and late into the evening, individual MLAs to convey the party high command's wishes in favour of Jogi.

But his miseries did not end there. Greater insult awaited him. On 1 November 2000, Digvijay Singh, as Chief Minister of the just-divided Madhya Pradesh, was physically attacked along with two Congress observers—Prabha Rau and Ghulam Nabi Azad—when they had gone to meet VC Shukla at his residence in the afternoon. Shukla had invited some select journalists to his farm house 'Radheshyam Bhavan' for lunch. I was there to witness the horrible incident that preceded the lunch. No sooner had the Congress leaders entered the sprawling and idyllic mansion of Shukla than the former health minister Ashok Rao and his followers pounced on Digvijay and hit him as he alighted from his official car. They hit him badly. In the ensuing chaos and melee, his white kurta was

Darkness at Noon    153

torn as he scampered for shelter into the drawing room. As it turned out, Shukla's supporters had resorted to this dastardly act to vent their ire against Digvijay for supporting Jogi over their leader, little realising that he too was against it, but was given no option.

Later, when we joined Shukla for lunch and asked him about the incident, seasoned politician that he was, he feigned complete ignorance about what had just happened outside and ushered us to his dining table to have a sumptuous meal. The scribes spent an hour chatting about everything but Shukla showed no interest in the sordid episode. Digvijay and the other leaders also hurriedly left the place without making much ado about the attack. The next day's national newspapers were full of details of this shocking occurrence of a chief minister being bashed up and bruised in the presence of journalists.

VC Shukla, the tall and fair-complexioned doyen of Chhattisgarh, died following the worst-ever Naxal attack on a Congress rally in Bastar on 25 May 2013. He received grievous bullet injuries in the stomach and succumbed to them a week later in Delhi.

## MP's Own BSP: *Bijali, Sadak, Pani*

By the end of 2001, realisation was dawning upon the people of MP that they were not getting what they expected from their government that was serving its second term. There were no proper roads, power supply was erratic and unannounced load shedding did not even spare hospitals. The government supply of electricity for agriculture was woefully inadequate making farmers angry. Rather than sympathising with people, Digvijay once advised them to "get habituated to such frequent cuts." Across MP, the demand for Diesel Generating sets and domestic inverters shot up. Senior political columnist of Delhi, Aditi Phadnis, wrote in a book brought out by *Business Standard* titled '*Political Profiles of Cabals and Kings*': "Ahead of the MP Assembly election in 2003, *Nai Duniya*, one of the state's best known Hindi newspapers published a letter to the Editor, which roughly translated ran like this: 'Dear editor, I feel that if there is an award for world's best genetic engineer, it should go to our Chief Minister Digvijay Singh. Power cuts are so prolonged in our State these days that soon there will be a whole generation of children who will have developed the capacity to see in the dark. Just as the giraffe grew a long neck partly as a mechanism for survival, our children too will have to teach themselves to read in the dark in order to survive. So, Mr Singh should be congratulated for creating conditions to introduce a new gene in human beings, yours, etc'."

A former bureaucrat and a well-known figure of Bhopal, MN Buch, wrote a series of hard-hitting articles in *Hindustan Times* Bhopal, on Digvijay's tenure saying that just nothing was going right in MP, be it education or urban infrastructure; agriculture or administration. *Jyotirma tamaso gamaya* was the title of one piece that meant... from the light lead us to darkness.

On his part, Digvijay, a great human being for ordinary people (if not for politicians), had set up what was called district governments in 61 districts of the undivided state on 1 April 1999. He had a State Act passed in the Assembly in 1995 that enabled the state government to delegate any of its works to district governments and district planning committees. It was his way of empowering people and decentralising power. In a speech he said, "I am happy to inform you that our Prime Minister Shri Atal Bihari Vajpayee has also commended this novel initiative...the results of this experiment are being awaited by the country."

The experiment, however, did not cut much ice with people.

## The Dalit Agenda

As the election loomed on the horizon, Digvijay and his worthy advisers came up with a scheme for the upliftment of Dalits, clearly to distract people from his poor governance and to lure a large share of votes from the downtrodden class that was close to 45-50%. It was also done to pre-empt the possible damage by the Bahujan Samaj Party (BSP) that had sent many MLAs to the Assembly in 1993.

Digvijay Singh termed it as Madhya Pradesh Model of Development. This preceded an all-India Dalit Conference in Bhopal in January 2002, convened under the direction of a young Dalit writer, Chandrabhan Prasad. In the government, two IAS officers close to the Chief Minister, Principal Secretary RN Berwa (CM's first appointment in 1993), and Secretary Amar Singh were seen as the architects of the Dalit Agenda.

The recommendations and conclusions of the India Dalit Intellectuals Conference at Bhopal was called the Bhopal Document. The 161-page document was published by the MP government in which Digvijay Singh wrote a lengthy yet scholarly article explaining his new-found ideology for the Dalits.

A few paragraphs (not in sequence but without much change in the context of his Dalit Agenda) read thus: "Dalits do not have a recorded history. A mass of 250 million outcasts comprising the untouchables and the tribals are grappling with history and survival at the turn of the millennium. The Indian society is made up of four *varnas* and *avarnas* comprising untouchables and the tribals apart from the minorities. Untouchables and tribals together termed as Dalits have always been outside the *varna* system. The untouchables remained a part of the village economy but were segregated to remain outside the village and perform menial services. Untouchables, during the course of time, were denied civil rights including the right to possess wealth, to acquire knowledge and possess arms...." Is half-a-century not enough to wipe out the dark spots from our civilisation? Haven't societies in our own continent—countries of East Asia—redefined their destinies and are on a fast-track of development today?"

Then talking about his pet model, Digvijay said: "But the State under the MP model of development assigned itself a role hitherto very reluctantly pursued in India. Madhya Pradesh model opens up a new channel of communication with the society. Considering the existing social dominance, the state is pursuing society to turn equitable on its own lest the society at large plunge into a more vicious cycle of tensions as being experienced in UP and Bihar... One of the finest examples of this new endeavour is our recent decision to reduce the percentage of grazing land/common land from 7.5% to 2% thus allotting 2/3rd of the total grazing land to SC/ST landless agricultural labourers...as a result four lakh acres of agriculture land is now available to landless SC/ST agricultural labourers."

However, at one point Digvijay wrote a politically loaded line, "We may like them, we may hate them but we cannot ignore them," and that adequately explains his real political agenda.

The State Government then issued guidelines in black and white that detailed all legal provisions for securing arms licences, for reservations, for issuance of various caste certificates, for appointments on compassionate grounds, for private medical college seats, for allotment of government houses to Dalits and so on. Bureaucrats were asked to be more sensitive in dealing with matters related to the Dalits and go the extra mile to ensure that the Dalit Agenda was implemented in letter and spirit.

While implementing the programme many collectors faced

tough opposition as an unholy alliance between the OBCs and the upper caste groups thwarted the government's efforts. Districts like Sehore, Indore, Rajgarh and parts of Malwa witnessed tensions. In Rajgarh, for instance, where the Dalit population was close to 21-22%, the collector and SP (JN Kansotiya and Sai Manohar) were attacked by a mob when they went to inspect damages to the standing crop of the Dalits on the land allotted by the State Government under the Dalit Agenda. The personal guard of the SP was seriously injured. Such was the anger of people across the state.

In the context of Shivraj Singh's governance pattern which I have mentioned earlier in the book, when we look back, the Digvijay 'model' actually created deep fissures in the society in Madhya Pradesh. Rural Madhya Pradesh was very tense; upper castes took umbrage at the fact that acres and acres of village common lands were being 'unjustifiably' given to scheduled castes and tribes just to win votes. At one point it seemed that Madhya Pradesh was going deep into an abyss.

The State Government, replacing its 1982 policy, brought out a new version 'The MP Environment Policy,1999' (Madhya Pradesh Rajya Paryavaran Neeti,1999) tabled in the State Assembly by Housing and Environment Minister Indrajeet Kumar on 16 March 1999. This stated that the common grazing land (*charnoi bhoomi*) would be conserved. But in one shot, under the Dalit Agenda, it was brought down to just 2% from 7.5%. This opened a pandora's box and led to unending social strife. The Dalits did not benefit as envisaged and the OBCs turned completely against the Congress government. Realising the turn of events, Digvijay Singh's younger brother Laxman Singh spoke against the model, perhaps because his constituency of Rajgarh was worst hit due to this pro-Dalit programme. One Dalit IAS field officer posted in Bhopal then

## 158 *Shivraj Singh And Rise Of Madhya Pradesh*

candidly told me that Digvijay Singh had gone a little too far to woo Dalits and this would not help him as some Dalit collectors, while enforcing the Dalit Agenda, reminded people of the Emergency excesses. In the bureaucracy too, divisions along caste lines became evident. There were two groups—one led by Berwa-Amar Singh and the other of non-Dalit officers. Upper caste officials and citizens alike were a frightened lot. But none had the courage to tell Digvijay Singh that he was pushing MP into the Dark Age and the society stood divided due to his imprudent policies. I felt it was darkness at noon!

Scholar and researcher Sudha Pai (2010) who dedicated a complete book to this Dalit Agenda experiment in MP, wrote: "The legacy of radical programmes and linkages with the lower castes/classes was taken forward by Digvijay Singh when the party (Congress) came to power. He was driven by both the political imperative to sustain the base of the party among these social groups and, as the many programmes implemented during his tenure indicate, a commitment to improve their socio-economic condition. The Dalit Agenda therefore was a strategy of 'political containment' on the part of the Digvijay Singh government, that is, an attempt to retain the support of Dalits/tribals in MP during a period of a strong wave of Dalit assertion in the Hindi heartland, led by the Bahujan Samaj Party (BSP)."

Pai quotes Shashank Kela (2003) who critically argued that while Digvijay Singh introduced a number of programmes such as Panchayati Raj, the Education Guarantee Scheme and land distribution, his government introduced no real change at ground level for the people.

Pai observes further: "Analysis of the electoral campaign of 2003 suggests that the Dalit Agenda, particularly the land distribution programme, contributed significantly to the defeat of the Congress

*Darkness at Noon* 159

Party at least in some parts of the state."

No surprise then that the upsurge and frenzy of people ousted the Digvijay Singh government and installed the BJP with a massive majority in November 2003—a year and a half after the Dalit Agenda was fully unfolded before the people.

It turned out to be a kind of poetic justice that riding the wave of this historic success was an OBC woman from the backwaters of Bundelkhand: Uma Bharti.

ଔଔଔ

Chapter - 12

# BJP: WINNING STROKES

Though election to the State Assembly was slated for November 2013, the BJP and its star performer, Shivraj, had already begun drawing meticulous plans months ahead of its traditional opponents. The Congress, like an ambling elephant, took its own time to stride ahead.

Shivraj was assiduously handling the government front rolling out populist welfare schemes in quick succession like a seasoned magician taking off his hat to release a white pigeon into the sky; moments later pulling out a fluffy rabbit and before the public could emerge from the spell, showing yet another trick to keep the audience applauding.

But Shivraj was clearly not entertaining people, he meant business—serious business at that. For very high stakes were involved, for him individually and for the party he was leading towards a new record. The schemes or projects he announced or official measures he took were all for the actual benefit of the people, to improve their lot—socially and economically. That obviously translated into a large number of votes as the election results went on to prove. His credibility as a performer par excellence was established again. Independent observers, however, maintain that a common

162 *Shivraj Singh And Rise Of Madhya Pradesh*

thread ran through the party's performance in four states, of which three went to the BJP and the fourth, Delhi, choosing the BJP as the largest single party ahead of Arvind Kejriwal's newly-formed Aam Aadmi Party (AAP). Was Narendra Modi's charisma attracting a large number of youth to the BJP, especially the first-time voters? Prasanna Sharma, a former Akhil Bhartiya Vidyarthi Parishad (ABVP) office-bearer who now runs 'Srijan', a Bhopal-based NGO for improving the technical education scenario, claims to have spoken to a large number of college students of Bhopal, who told him "they were voting for Modi," regardless of the fact that the elections were for the MP Assembly. *DNA*, an English newspaper from Jaipur, also reported on 9 December 2013 that it was the Modi factor that helped the BJP in all the four states.

Many leaders unofficially maintain that if the BJP came back to power with such a thumping majority, the Modi factor was relevant. But that does not belittle in any way the eight-year-old tenure of the MP Chief Minister—his contribution to the overall development of his state and his popularity, something the Congress leader, Jyotiraditya Scindia, also conceded on the day of the results. In his interviews to the media he admitted (after his party's severe drubbing) that "Congress lost to Shivraj's popularity".

The BJP did not depend on its government's performance alone. The government's public relations department unleashed a blitzkrieg of high value advertisements of various government schemes on the one hand with the party apparatus doing its bit on the other. As early as on 25 February 2013, BJP launched its "Maha Jansampark Abhiyan (mass people contact campaign), timing it well with Sant Ravidas Jayanti. Sant Ravidas was the 15th-16th century socio-religious reformist from a lower caste and is worshipped in north India, Maharashtra and parts of central India. He was opposed to the social untouchability among castes. By launching the campaign from Bhopal that day, Shivraj Singh gave a loud and clear message to the downtrodden; party chief Narendra Singh Tomar simultaneously flagged off the campaign from Gwalior and organization general secretary Arvind Menon did it from Indore, the same day. Ravidas Jayanti is a government holiday in MP for many years now.

While in Bhopal the Chief Minister and his team were working round the clock, either at his picturesque Shyamla Hills official residence, overlooking the 1,000 year-old, man-made Upper Lake or at the Deendayal Parisar (BJP state headquarters in Arera Colony). His trusted bureaucrats, Chief Secretary R Parshuram (who was given extension of service for six months), Principal Secretary Manoj Shrivastava, secretaries SK Mishra and Hari Ranjan Rao, besides a few secretaries of key departments, like energy, PWD, public relations and agriculture, were racing against time to achieve the set targets. "I don't think there is anything that would stop this government from coming back to power," SK Mishra had told me at an industrialist's party in Indore, sometime in March-April that year.

The party machinery was busy screening the list of nominees and sending people to various Assembly segments for ground surveys or 'rai shumari'. Surveys were multi-pronged and scientific, Anil Dave who was in charge of the exercise for the past three elections informed me. How did it work? Well, a single-sheet format in each of the 230 constituencies was distributed to those who were either present office bearers or former MLAs, panchayat representatives or local party officials. In each constituency 70 such forms were distributed in which probable/winning candidates' names were asked to be marked. But it had a rider—the person filling the form could not write his or her name; secondly, no blood relative was to be recommended. After the forms were collected through the

## 164 *Shivraj Singh And Rise Of Madhya Pradesh*

district units, the individuals named in it were given marks on priority, ie. in how many of the 70 forms one person stood as the first choice and another as second. Following this *rai shumari*, the BJP screening committee would apply other parameters such as the candidate's character, standing in the society, caste background and number of local voters of his caste, State intelligence inputs, and so on. Candidates thus emerged, Dave claims, and were recommended to the Central Election Committee in Delhi and only winnable candidates got tickets barring few exceptions. He, however, concedes that at least 20 'self-goals' (wrong tickets) were made by the BJP in ticket distribution or else the tally would have gone up to 185.

A number of pro-poor schemes, schemes for women and the girl child were already implemented in 2011-12 and people were deriving benefits from them. As far as gender representation is concerned, the BJP gave tickets to 28 women candidates out of whom 22 won. From the Congress, only six of the 21 fielded could enter the hallowed precincts of the State Assembly, a fact that shows how the BJP and its government went about its business methodically. Women and girl child welfare was the party and government's main plank in these elections besides agricultural growth. Simultaneously, ad-agencies and other coordinators were working on different plans to woo voters by showcasing government's achievements in many sectors. Close to 70 schemes were running parallel to each other and all were publicised profusely. Such a high-value advertisement campaign had never been witnessed before in MP.

All this had begun in April-May 2013 or even before. Devendra Malviya, Managing Director of the Midas Touch, an Indore-based creative advertising firm, told me that his first presentation was done in April 2013 in front of the concerned government officials and the CM. He also bagged the contract for a short documentary and creative ads shown in newspapers and TV during the campaign time.

Work was clearly divided and specific jobs assigned. Dave, a Rajya Sabha member and a key strategist and planner of '*Javli*'—a kind of war room first made in Bhopal in 2003 to take on the might of 10-year-old Digvijay Singh regime—was in charge of the CM's Jan Ashirwad Yatra this time round, besides other major meetings, including that of Narendra Modi at Bhopal.

Javli, a thick forested area near Mahabaleshwar valley in Maharashtra was historically famous as the much venerated warrior Maratha king Shivaji Maharaj Bhosale (1630-1680) had selected it for planning his major war strategy against the Muslim army. Those in the BJP who thought of this concept during the 2003 battle against Congress later disbanded the Javli team and left the place in Bhopal after their record-setting victory. But the experience did help the BJP this time too. A little change was there. Then it was a strategic team led by firebrand Uma Bharti but 10 years down the line it was the modest magician Shivraj's smooth working, hand in hand with Narenda Singh Tomar and Arvind Menon. Uma was out of the frame. During all the three elections (2003, 2008, 2013) Anil Dave played the significant role of a backroom boy, although strategic dimensions kept changing every five years. As part of their multi-pronged strategy, the BJP denied tickets to as many as 47 sitting MLAs including three ministers this time.

I remember one of the BJP's sitting MLAs had come to see the CM with a request for a transfer many days before the elections. He repeatedly pleaded that if a particular officer was posted in his constituency, he would win the election hands down, at which the CM quickly asked, "If you are so confident of that officer, why not give the BJP ticket to him rather than to you?" Needless to say, the MLA was dumbfounded and returned empty-handed.

## 166 *Shivraj Singh And Rise Of Madhya Pradesh*

Shivraj knew everything about all the constituencies and their local permutations and combinations, thanks to his constant touch with people and his visits to various places.

## Modi's Rallies

Modi addressed a number of rallies in Madhya Pradesh but one that stands out and underlines BJP's advanced preparations was at Bhopal. It was party ideologue Pt Deendayal Upadhyay's 97th birth anniversary. A mammoth rally of booth workers in Bhopal was held on 18th October, in which, according to high ranking police officials, close to three lakh already identified booth workers of the party across MP—and not the general rank and file—had gathered. The party had targeted to collect five lakh booth volunteers the rally in-charge Dave, an environmentalist had told me at his house, " *Nadi Ka Ghar*" (a river's home) a week ahead of the massive gathering. It was in this rally that Modi reiterated his 'Congress-free nation' slogan more forcefully and urged upon the people to rid Madhya Pradesh of the Congress (Congress-*mukt* MP). Interestingly, 16 of 51 districts in MP now do not have a single MLA elected on the *panja* (human hand/palm) symbol. The booth workers' meeting at the Jamboree ground was a great hit to the extent that the party had sought entry into the *Guinness Book of World Records* as one of the biggest political rallies.

Modi also addressed 15 public meetings in Satna, Indore, Sagar and Gwalior to name a few major places. Everywhere, he drew large crowds consisting mainly of the youth who spontaneously thronged the venues to listen to the aggressive orator and to feel the magnetic personality of the strong leader.

Surprisingly, the Congress had no inkling of this plan of the BJP to mobilise its committed workers and assign them specific tasks on the day of polling. Busy as they were, fighting relentlessly among themselves, they could not take a leaf out of BJP's book. A glaring example of their woolly thinking!

A little more comparison between the challenger Congress and the defender BJP would be apt here: Shivraj Singh Chouhan set out on his 'Jan Ashirwad Yatra' on 22 July, 2013 from Ujjain, with his bête noire Prabhat Jha with him on the chariot. Jha was angry and sullen having lost his prime position. "But a clever Shivraj kept him along all through the *yatra,* to prevent Jha from causing any damage to him or the party," a senior party functionary analysed it for me. The *Yatra* culminated in Indore on 4 October and generated fairly good response.

Shivraj Singh alone addressed 143 election rallies and meetings followed by Uma Bharti, Rajnath Singh, Sushma Swaraj, Nitin Gadkari, Arun Jaitley and LK Advani.

The Congress, on the other hand, half-heartedly announced Scindia as their campaign committee chief along with other teams like election committee, manifesto committee etc. as late as on 3 September 2013. The party's election committee meetings in Delhi were held on 7, 18 and 22 September and the screening committee kept working till 8 November—cutting and adding names as per the pulls and pressures of senior leaders. The Congress shied away from projecting Scindia as the prospective chief minister, though the party high command, according to a cover story of *India Today* (dated 30 October 2013) had already taken a decision to this effect earlier in the year. True to Congress culture, it could not be implemented. An insider said that senior party politicians, wary of Scindia's popularity and positive image among the youth did their best to dissuade and delay Rahul Gandhi from making any formal announcement to make Scindia the face of the party against Shivraj.

#### 168 *Shivraj Singh And Rise Of Madhya Pradesh*

This indeed cost the Congress dear though no one in the party's higher echelons conceded it openly, barring Satyavrat Chaturvedi who was the first to blast Digvijay Singh. Chaturvedi said Scindia should have been named much earlier.

Thanks to their infighting, Scindia could hold his first meeting at the PCC office in mid-September at Bhopal and it turned out to be perhaps his last. While all the top Congress leaders did travel to many places for election meetings and tried their best to portray their 'unity', at the ground level, there was no stopping the dissidence and hurling of open charges against each other. To add insult to injury, PCC chief and former Union Minister, Kantilal Bhuria, a tribal from Jhabua, on the Gujarat border, did not have a pan-Madhya Pradesh presence or mass appeal. He quit the Tribal Welfare Ministry in April 2012 and was made the party boss by the AICC. But with his limited political acumen and stature, and almost zero organising capability, compared to his counterpart Narendra Singh Tomar, poor Bhuria could not deliver what was expected of a PCC chief in an election year, rued a former minister from Mandsaur. The tribal card the Congress tried to play through him simply did not click in MP where the tribal population is one crore.

Bhuria has always been a close follower of Digvijay Singh, who was instrumental in making him first the Union Minister of the important tribal ministry with huge budgetary allocations, and later had him nominated as the PCC chief a year before the state elections. After the humiliating defeat, Bhuria was axed by the Congress on 13 January 2014. A younger MP from Khandwa, Arun Yadav, son of former Deputy Chief Minister (late) Subhash Yadav, an adversary of Digvijay Singh in his heyday was nominated as PCC chief, clearly with an eye on the youth during the forthcoming Lok Sabha elections. Incidentally, it was Subhash Yadav as PCC chief (2004-

2008) who had obtained some kind of a permission from the AICC that senior leaders would not enter MP to hold any political meeting without explicit permission of the Pradesh Congress Committee. PCC had issued this kind of a written directive to restrain 'vocal leaders' who Yadav thought would damage the party through their statements rather than doing any good.

During the 2013 election campaign, Digvijay Singh who shot into limelight with his politically-loaded *'doobta suraj'* (setting sun) comment at a Rahul Gandhi rally in Gwalior, was the natural choice from Rajgarh which he had represented in Parliament. But he preferred to enter it through what is called in colloquial political parlance the 'back door'—the Rajya Sabha—on 27 January 2014, for six straight years. What he had meant in Gwalior was that he was a 'setting sun' in politics; he was also on record saying earlier that he did not favour entering the *Sansad* (Parliament) through the back door.

In Delhi, while the Congress leaders Digvijay Singh (AICC general secretary), Union Ministers Kamal Nath and Jyotiraditya Scindia, PCC chief Bhuria, AICC general secretary in charge of the state Mohan Prakash, Satyavrat Chaturvedi, an RS member and AICC spokesman, and State leaders Suresh Pachauri and Ajay Singh, the leader of the Opposition in state Assembly, could not even hold one serious official meeting together about the impending elections strategy, selection of candidates or planning an aggressive and convincing advertisement campaign, the BJP had almost completed two rounds of homework for all 230 constituencies. Its strategy of projecting Shivraj was already in place and a number of imaginative advertisements were ready to be released. Their party apparatus, led by Narendra Tomar (an upper caste Thakur who became president of the State unit for the second time in December 2012 in a very

*170 Shivraj Singh And Rise Of Madhya Pradesh*

closely guarded move by CM's trusted people), worked like a well-oiled machine, round the clock. He camped in Bhopal for months together and toured when required to different districts for party meetings. Tomar is known to be a low profile, non-controversial leader but an excellent organiser. He also shares a very old and friendly relationship with Shivraj, and that is why the state BJP did not have to look up to Delhi every now and then.

How shrewd a politician is Shivraj? Some people say he is as shrewd as any other top politician, while a section in the BJP believes that he is a straight forward politician and does not scheme and plot against his rivals. His political shrewdness came in sharp focus during the Prabhat Jha episode. When the ambitious Jha, having completed his two-year term, was preparing for the second, as president in December 2012, he was hoisted with his own petard. Prabhat was once the media in-charge under state unit chief Vikram Verma—among the most simple and straight forward leaders of the party. Jha never belonged to the CM camp but managed to grab the key position through his proximity to RSS senior functionary Suresh Soni who had his say in many things in MP. Soni had first discussed the issue with the CM in Chhindwara at a BJP function, according to top sources. And he later spoke with Tomar who knew Prabhat well, both being from the same city. When finally Tomar, then in charge of Uttar Pradesh BJP affairs, agreed to talk to Shivraj he is said to have told Soni that without using his name (Soni's) it would not be possible to elevate Jha to that position.

When Prabhat's name was almost finalised in Delhi for the first time in 2010, a journalist friend in my presence held the CM's hand firmly in the latter's fifth-floor office in the state secretariat and gave him a friendly suggestion: "Please don't let Jha become party chief as he will prove to be a serious threat to you." CM had just nodded his head but could do little to stop Jha then.

One senior BJP leader told me on condition of anonymity that when Prabhat was finally made the State unit president despite opposition from all senior leaders, the relationship between the BJP and the RSS was not very cordial and refusal to make an RSS nominee the State unit chief would have further strained the ties. Shivraj clearly was not in a mood to add fuel to the fire by antagonising the RSS further. He adopted a conciliatory approach. But meanwhile, an ill-prepared Sumitra Mahajan threatened to contest as she, like Kailash Joshi, Sunderlal Patwa, Vikram Verma, was opposed to Jha. After a little tension at the BJP office, she was persuaded to withdraw and Jha became the president.

Things then started happening exactly the way the journalist had warned Shivraj. Jha became a rallying point for all anti-Shivraj ministers, including controversial Kailash Vijayvargiya, easily among the most 'resourceful' ministers of the Shivraj cabinet. Once close friends, their relationship soured over the years as Vijayvargiya also wanted to be the CM and did everything possible to make it happen. Shivraj, on his own, did not do much to damage Kailash, though people expected him to be tough on his minister who faced many charges.

Having completed a year in office, Jha pestered party leaders and also the CM to organise a function to felicitate himself at the CM house. This was unprecedented and BJP became a laughing stock in the eyes of the people but Jha got it done and the CM kept giving him a long rope. The 'grand felicitation' of a BJP state unit president, with no great achievements under his belt, took place at Shaymla Hills. Shivraj does not agree on record that it was against his wishes that he had to 'felicitate' Jha but deep within he was unwilling to be host at such a function.

172 *Shivraj Singh And Rise Of Madhya Pradesh*

Shivraj could not prevent Jha from becoming the state president for the first term but during the second term he kept his cards close to his chest and played them very astutely in the nick of time and denied Jha the second term. Just as the second term's official election process began within the party, Shivraj swung into action. Leaders like Vikram Verma and Sumitra Mahajan (seven-time MP from Indore without a defeat) both committed party veterans with clean image, quietly worked out a plan. They took a few more leaders along without Jha getting wind of it and proposed Narendra Singh Tomar's name in place of Jha's when the latter was fully assured of a smooth second innings.

Tomar was in Odisha on the eve of filing nomination and had no inkling what was happening in Bhopal. "When I was in charge of UP, I had stopped looking back at MP and just did not dabble there," he told me once. He got a call from party president Nitin Gadkari to rush to Delhi on 14 December to meet him. After the meeting, Tomar was asked to go to Bhopal on 15 December to file the nomination for the 16 December 2012 election. In the meantime, when Gadkari had asked Shivraj, he had very confidentially told Gadkari that in the election year he would not settle for anyone but the tried and tested Tomar. Tomar was elected unanimously as none was there to support Jha and Tomar had the backing of everyone, including Suresh Soni of the RSS who did not press for his protégé's name again.

During the charge-taking function of the new president at BJP state headquarters, Jha in presence of the CM, Tomar and many senior leaders, exploded: "The secrecy that shrouded my removal was matching the secrecy of Pokhran blasts during Atalji's time." With a powerful Sangh lobby backing him, Jha never ever dreamt of such an inglorious and sudden ouster. What he did not realise is that Shivraj had done his *jamawat* (setting) very secretly in Delhi with the RSS and the BJP too. With one stroke, he exhibited how shrewd a leader he could be, if things came anywhere close to his own survival. Incidentally, both Tomar and Jha come from Gwalior, a BJP bastion since Rajmata Vijayaraje Scindia's days. Both have a strong mutual dislike for each other.

Once Tomar was firmly in the saddle, Shivraj became more confident of the party's victory. His and Tomar's understanding, political thinking and strategising abilities are in great sync. With organisation secretary Arvind Menon, the trio had done much of the ground work many months ahead of the actual poll preparations. In 2008, the same Singh-Tomar duo had worked in tandem to help the BJP retain power with 143 seats and a higher percentage of vote share. Govind Maloo, a former party spokesman and vice-chairman of a State Government undertaking said that during the run-up to elections, an election cell was set up at the party office which was closely monitoring all the campaigns, requirements of candidates such as a top leader's rally, fund management, caste issues or sabotage complaints or anything like that in all 230 seats. "If something was amiss somewhere, it would be brought to the CM or Tomar's knowledge who would quickly fix things—be it resources or caste equations or whatever," Maloo said, adding "we used to work till late into the nights with Ananth Kumar sitting there with us."

## Congress Factionalism

Such genuine bonhomie among top BJP leaders was quite alien to the Congress. Also, it did not have the organisational structure and skills to take on the BJP. "We lost due to total collapse of organisation at the state level as also at the district and block levels, besides the fierce infighting," admitted PCC general secretary Govind Goyal

174 *Shivraj Singh And Rise Of Madhya Pradesh*

to me in my office after about a month of the Congress rout. Goyal lost by 70,644 votes from Bhopal's Govindpura constituency. The winner Babulal Gaur, 85, posted his 10th straight victory, a rare electoral record in the country. Gaur had been replaced by Shivraj Singh Chouhan as CM in 2005. In Gaur's first election, Shivraj had worked as a volunteer and today Shivraj, 30 years younger to Gaur, is his boss. That is politics!

But then Congress factionalism was not new to the party members or the people. In the absence of any formidable opposition, the Congress had continued to rule over MP in the past decades. Sudha Pai, a social scientist from the JNU, notes in her book, *Developmental State And The Dalit Question in Madhya Pradesh: Congress Response* that factionalism proved too deep-seated to be removed. In the 1962 State Assembly elections, the Congress obtained only 142 seats. An investigation by the Congress high command pointed to internal sabotage by leaders of disaffected factional groups who had supported Opposition candidates. Eventually, the central leadership appointed DP Mishra as the Chief Minister in 1963 and he was able to unite the warring factions, as a result of which the Congress performed better in 1967 elections." Ms Pai, quoting R Chandidas and others, says (while referring to factionalism and establishment of a two-party system), "Although Congress improved its position and gained 167 seats, the emerging structure of bi-partisanship in the state is clearly seen in the 1967 elections. Owing to the failure of the Congress to extend beyond its core areas, the Jan Sangh had managed to (gradually) improve its position from a mere six seats in 1952 to 78 in 1967." Quoting Wayne Wilcox, she further observes: "Factionalism along regional lines in MP was a product of existence of a number of disparate regions that were part of CPs and were put together to form the new state in 1956. Wilcox had recognised that integrating the party was a difficult task as factionalism was a long-standing phenomenon."

Despite factionalism, the Congress continued to rule many Indian states as also the country for decades together. In MP, the first non-Congress government came to power in 1977, post Emergency in the shape of Janata Party but it did not last its full term.

Coming back to 2013, it can be safely said that the Congress got ready just about three months ahead of the crucial polls and tried in vain to get its act together. While BJP's chief ministerial candidate was well-known much before the two parties got into poll mode, the Congress was confused whether to project Scindia or not. Finally, when they declared Scindia willy-nilly as campaign committee chief, it was too late in the day. Scindia, despite his 'Mr. Clean' image and extreme hard work could do little for his party.

It was public knowledge that Congress leaders had their outsize egoes coming in the way. Therefore, they had to repeatedly show that 'they were one' by coming on the stage hand in hand. Soon after a public rally, they would go in their own respective directions for campaigning. That they travelled a number of times together did not cut much ice with voters who, by now, knew their internal differences far too well.

What also contributed to the debacle was the Congress Party's inexplicable decision to navigate the party from Delhi rather than their leaders camping for over a month and a half in Bhopal. At a lunch hosted by Narendra Singh Tomar for the mediapersons in January, Shivraj was heard ridiculing Congress leaders' style of 'coming to MP in the morning and going back to Delhi in the night'.

Those who saw and covered these elections from close say that Divvijay Singh was the biggest spoil sport in the 2013 elections. "If the Congress did not come to power in MP, the lion's share of the blame goes to this Singh (Digvijay)," Congressmen openly complained, wondering why the party high command did not see this.

Chandrakant Naidu, a former regional editor of *Hindustan Times*, wrote in Delhi's *Outlook* magazine (dated 25 November, 2013): A large chunk of the hate mail flooding the Madhya Pradesh Congress inbox is addressed to former Chief Minister Digvijay Singh. On social networking sites, his first name invokes carnivorous puns from supporters of the BJP. Naidu went on to write, quoting an unnamed former follower (of Digvijay), "Shocking that the BJP should be calling him names when it owes him its 10 years in power." Naidu concludes his beautiful piece on Digvijay: "Hard to say if he can contribute much to Congress progress but, if offended, he can harm the party more than its enemies."

BJP's well-designed and appealing campaign of 2003 in which Digvijay Singh was dubbed as 'Shriman Bantadhar' (Mr Disaster) was reused with fine improvements, to remind people that if he and his party returned to power in the state, MP's growth would instantly halt, as was witnessed during the 10 years of his rule (from 1993-2003).

Perhaps MP voters did not want the Congress to come out of the Raghogarh doghouse! The Bantadhar campaign was such a success among people across the huge state that middle class families were heard openly talking against Digvijay and his lack of governance. The campaign was aimed at scaring citizens of MP that if he (Digvijay Singh) came back to rule, directly or indirectly, the state would be ruined all over again. If there was some dislike in people's mind for him, BJP's constant hammering through a series of advertisements and speeches turned it into widespread hatred, exactly the way Indians had started hating former Prime Minister

VP Singh after he implemented the recommendations of the Mandal Commission.

Party workers blame him (Digvijay) for everything after the loss. He did whatever was possible to check Scindia in his tracks and managed Congress tickets in such a way that those whom he wanted won, in the strong Shivraj wave. They included his son Jaivardhan Singh, a smart and intelligent young man from the family pocket-borough Raghogarh in district Guna. Incidentally, Guna is also the Lok Sabha constituency of Scindia who is a third-time MP from there. Jaiwardhan made his debut this time from Raghogarh, a tiny royal state under the erstwhile large fiefdom of the Scindias. (In Marathi, the Maratha royal family was always known as Shinde, their original surname which over the past 100 years or so was anglicised to Scindia.)

From Raghogarh's adjoining constituency of Chachoda (which Digvijay had won in 1994 by-elections), about 30 km away, the BJP won comfortably. Some Congressmen say Shiv Narayan Meena, the sitting MLA, was reluctant to contest but Digvijay had reportedly taken upon himself the responsibility to help Meena retain the seat. In Guna district, the Congress won only two of the four seats.

Rajya Sabha member and senior Congress Party spokesman in Delhi Satyavrat Chatrurvedi is on record (*Dainik Bhaskar* dated 10.12.13) castigating Digvijay and blaming him for the Congress rout. So was Mahidpur (Ujjain) MLA Kalpana Parulekar who lost. In a telephonic conversation with the author, Chaturvedi shared his take on Chattarpur district near the famous temple town of Khajuraho in Bundelkhand. Of the six Assembly segments (seats) in the district, the BJP won five and the Congress bagged one. Not a surprise, at a time when the 'Shivraj wave' was sweeping across the state. How did this sixth go the Congress's way? According to Chaturvedi, it

178  *Shivraj Singh And Rise Of Madhya Pradesh*

was because the local Congress candidate Vikram Singh had put his foot down that he did not want Digvijay to hold a single meeting or else he would lose. That is precisely what happened! Digvijay campaigned in all five segments of Maharajpur, Chandla, Bijawar, Chhattarpur and Bada Malhara and could not (or did not) go to Rajnagar. Barring the Rajnagar candidate of the Congress, all others lost but Vikram Singh 'Natiraja' managed to defeat the Agriculture Welfare and Development Minister, Dr Ramkrishna Kusumariya, who had shifted from Patharia (Damoh district) to Rajnagar taking it to be a 'safe seat'. And he lost at a time when his department (agriculture) had done exceedingly well across the state winning awards at the national level. The minister of state for agriculture too lost from another constituency. It was a strange coincidence.

There could be other reasons too, but Vikram Singh surprisingly beat the anti-incumbency factor and registered a third straight win from the same constituency!

The story of Congress ignominy, however, does not end here. It also shows that having displayed their 'unity', some senior leaders also indirectly put up their candidates as 'rebels' and reportedly funded them to damage their own party's official candidate. This may be difficult to prove but there are constituencies where the losers complained that owing to such open rebellion at the behest of various leaders, they lost. In Indore-II constituency where sitting MLA and a close associate of Industries Minister Kailash Vijayvargiya, Ramesh Mendola's massive victory by over 90,000 votes, set the Indoreans tongues wagging, that 'Congress had deliberately fielded a very weak candidate like Chotu Shukla'. Shukla's name was finalised, after changing two names in quick succession, which according to independent observers had helped Vijayvargiya, who was fighting a tough battle in Mhow. He required the 'dada' (Mendola) to manage

BJP: Winning Strokes 179

voters by hook or by crook to ensure victory of his political mentor. Thus Chotu Shukla, having almost retired from active politics, was chosen by the Congress. Vijayvargiya won by a mere 12,000 votes against Antar Singh Durbar, as compared to his own protégé Mendola's 90,000 vote win. Vijayvargiya knew it was a tough battle and had tried his best to change his constituency but the party did not permit him to do so. He had wanted to shift to Indore-III, a safe BJP pocket from where Usha Thakur won by more votes than Vijayvargiya.

The fact remains that while the BJP had worked in a very systematic and scientific manner at every stage, the Congress's campaign, if there was any, had completely gone haywire. Their leaders did not trust each other; there were groups within groups and the ordinary Congress worker did not know how to combat BJP's well-orchestrated campaign all through and their offensive and convincing development plank. The top leaders—Rahul Gandhi, Scindia, Digvijay Singh, Kamal Nath—held public meetings but they fell short of the desired success.

In the Congress, there was no single person in command directing the operations. AICC general secretary Mohan Prakash, a well-meaning former socialist leader who was looking after the MP affairs, was too simple to understand the wheels within wheels. His counterpart Ananth Kumar, a former Union minister in the NDA government, was making repeated visits to Bhopal and other places and was pepping up the party rank and file. He had little problem working with the MP unit of the BJP, whereas the same could not be said about Mohan Prakash.

Curiously, while the BJP's main slogan on all the hoardings and publicity material for the election was '*Phir Bhajapa, Phir Shivraj*' (BJP again, Shivraj again), Congress's main campaigner Scindia was not only missing in the capital city's banners and posters but also from the party's official election manifesto covers. The party's official manifesto committee, headed by former Union Minister Suresh Pachauri, brought out the document which did not have Scindia's name or photo anywhere in it. Unity... Did one say ?

Incidentally, Pachauri too lost by over 20,000 votes from Bhojpur to Surendra Patwa, a sitting MLA and nephew of former CM Sunderlal Patwa.

ଔଔଔଔ

# EPILOGUE

I am not a great sympathiser of Shivraj Singh Chouhan nor all his ways of administration. I am neither his close friend, as he has very few in any case. I seldom meet him at his home or at functions. Yet, as a proud 'Madhya Pradeshi' I have witnessed (as a journalist of over 30 years' standing) in him a Chief Minister who has tried to do sincere work in the once BIMARU state. It may be debatable if the BIMARU tag has been finally removed from Madhya Pradesh, but yes, all indicators point towards that, barring the health sector. Despite all claims by health ministers and officials in the health department, Government hospitals are in a terrible shape. Top officers believe in constructing big buildings and purchasing expensive machines but providing satisfactory and genuine healthcare services are NOT being provided to poor patients—that doesn't seem to be anyone's priority. There is an issue of quality and reliability of service and treatment. Medicines procured and supplied are sub-standard and most doctors are insensitive towards patients, giving rise to a flourishing medical trade in the private sector. Upon his completion of five years in office as CM on 29 November 2010, in an interview to this author, Shivraj had admitted this fact saying, "A lot is required to be done in the health sector." Yet, four years down the line he is expected to focus his personal attention—like he did to agriculture—on this important basic service delivery in the interest of the poor people. Admittedly, he is one Chief Minister (without any bias towards any of his several predecessors), who came very close to being described unarguably as a true statesman, in letter and spirit and who has untiringly worked for the growth of MP.

Shivraj is no less a politician. In India we know what kind of politicians run the country and states barring a few notable exceptions. Shivraj too is afflicted by most of the shortcomings of an Indian politician. Yet, he is different. With all the conviction at my command, I can reiterate that he is committed to a cause—the cause of uplifting Madhya Pradesh.

The recent growth in agriculture and the fact that Indian MNCs such as Infosys and TCS thought of setting up their IT SEZs in Madhya Pradesh is a salute to the State Government's efforts to provide a responsive administration that attracted worthwhile investment among the competing Indian states in a global economy, at a time when a social revolution was also unfolding in MP.

Why this book? This question could well have been answered in the introduction but I deliberately avoided mentioning it there in great detail though I have touched upon it.

Madhya Pradesh and its politics is rarely discussed at the national level. I therefore thought of putting on record for posterity, the basic facts of the social transformation brought about by a Chief Minister who neither studied abroad nor came from a renowned political family. The BJP did not have deep roots in MP but the past decade amply shows that it has captured the people's imagination, thanks to Shivraj's overall performance. Contemporary politics and the role played by a Chief Minister in trying to turn around a state honestly needs some independent evaluation.

*Epilogue*  183

This is that brief evaluation which is in your hands.

In my long journalistic career I have seen a number of Chief Ministers of MP and other states. Some had great virtues and some did not; some were pure politicians while some had a sense of statesmanship. Shivraj falls under the latter category.

How history will treat Shivraj Singh Chouhan cannot be predicted now. Today even Pt Jawaharlal Nehru or Lal Bahadur Shastri or Narasimha Rao are not remembered adequately enough by the mobile phone apps-driven generation, so what about Shivraj? He too could be easily forgotten.

Luckily, he has not yet endeavoured to erect his own statues in Madhya Pradesh cities and towns like former UP Chief Minister Mayawati of the BSP, nor is he personally inclined to let his wife contest an election, though she is said to be harbouring some political ambitions according to media reports.

Having watched him closely for over 10 years, I definitely see a positive zeal in him to take Madhya Pradesh on the path of development through good governance (MP under him, won a prestigious United Nations Award at New York in June 2012 for the MP Public Service Guarantee Act under the UN's category of Improving the Delivery of Public Services), which was hitherto lacking! Corruption is of course an area where he would need to be far more tough than what he is today, though it might have its political fall-out. Yes, he did start Day One of his third innings with publicly declaring his policy of 'zero tolerance' for corruption.

My effort as a discerning citizen and watchful journalist has been to present the facts and analysis before the reader in my own modest way and with the understanding that I have at my disposal!

There have been, of late, several biographical books written on many regional satraps—Akhilesh Yadav, Nitish Kumar, Mulayam

Singh Yadav, Sharad Pawar, Sushil Kumar Shinde and of course Narendra Modi. Biographies of YB Chavan, Lal Bahadur Shastri, Indira Gandhi, Rajiv Gandhi and other top politicians are also available.

This is the first of its kind effort to put things in perspective about a lesser known state and its low profile Chief Minister.

I earnestly hope that some precious time may be devoted by policy makers, researchers, economists, political analysts, bureaucrats and diplomats to this central Indian state which has been largely ignored since its birth almost six decades ago.

CRCRCR

# REFERENCE

- Ashish Bose, *Headcount: Memoirs of a Demographer*; Penguin Books 2010.
- Daniel Lak, *Mantras of Change;* Penguin/Viking *2005.*
- MN Buch, *When the Harvest Moon is Blue*; Har-Anand Publications New Delhi 2008.
- Surinder Sud, *The Changing Profile of Indian Agriculture*; BS Books 2009.
- Sir Albert Howard, *An Agricultural Testament*; Other India Press Goa (first published 1940).
- Rajesh Shukla, Sunil Jain & Preeti Kakkar, *Caste in a Different Mould;* BS Books 2010.
- Nandan Nilekani, *Imagining India*; Penguin 2008.
- NR Narayana Murthy, *A Better India, A Better World*; Penguin 2009.
- Arun Sinha, *Nitish Kumar and Rise of Bihar*; Penguin/Viking 2011.
- Nilanjan Mukhopadhyay, *Narendra Modi*; Tranquebar 2013.
- Dilip Chaware, *Saga of a Struggle: Sushil Kumar Shinde* ; Chinar Publishers Pune 2008.
- Vir Sanghvi & Namita Bhandare, *Madhavrao Scindia: A Life*; Penguin/Viking 2009.

- Arun Shourie, *Governance and the Sclerosis that has set in*; Rupa 2004.
- Dom Moraes, *Answered by Flutes*; Asia Publishing House1983.
- Aditi Phadnis, *Political Profiles*; BS Books 2009.
- Anuj Gupt, *Battle of Hindi Heartland*; Anas Communications N Delhi 2003.
- Dr PL Mishra, *The Political Biography of Chhattsigarh*; Vishwa Bharti Prakashan Nagpur.
- Eds: Dominic Emmanuel, Francis Gonsalves, John Dayal, *The Other side: Redefining Bharat*; Vitasta Delhi 2010.
- Ed Samuel Paul, *Fighting Corruption: The Way forward*; Academic Foundation Delhi 2013.
- Ed NK Singh & Nicholas Stern, *The New Bihar: Rekindling Governance and Development*; Harper Collins 2013.
- Sudha Pai, *Developmental State and Dalit Question in MP*; Routledge 2010.
- Sunita Aron, *Akhilesh Yadav: Winds of Change*; Tranquebar 2013.
- Government of Madhya Pradesh, *The Bhopal Document: The Dalit Agenda;* Bhopal 2002.
- *India Today Weekly* (Annual State of State Reports); Delhi 2003-13.
- *Economic and Political Weekly* (06 January 2010; 30 January 2010).
- *Hindustan Times*-Bhopal and Delhi editions (28 July and 9 December, 2013).
- *Gross State Domestic Products figures*; CMIE Report.
- *Frontline Magazine*; 18 December 2009; 26 February 2010; Chennai.
- *Planning Commission Report*,12th five Year Plan; Chapter 11— Regional Equality.

Reference    187

- *Outlook Magazine*, 25 November 2013; New Delhi.
- *Madhya Pradesh Human Development Report*-2007, Oxford University Press.
- *Wikipedia*, The Free Encyclopedia.
- *From Your School to Our School*, Rajiv Gandhi Shiksha Mission Bhopal; August 2000.
- *Sunday Magazine*, 28 January-3 February 1996; Calcutta.
- *Data-book for use of Dy Chairman*, Planning Commission-18 December. 2013 (http://planningcommission.gov.in).
- Sanjoy Bagchi, *The Changing Face of Bureaucracy*; Rupa & Co 2007.
- Bhaskar Ghose, *The Service Of The State – IAS Reconsidered*; Penguin 2011.
- LP Singh, *Portrait of Lal Bahadur Shastri-A Quintessential Gandhian*; Ravi Dayal Publisher, N Delhi 1996.
- Ed by LN Rangrajan, *Kautilya, The Arthashatra*; Penguin Classic 1990.
- Shaharyar M. Khan, *Begums of Bhopal — A Dynasty of Women in Raj India*; Viva Books Private Ltd.
- Asim Chaushuri, *Vivekananda: A Born Leader*; Advaita Ashram, Uttarakhand

## Hindi

- Deepak Tiwari, *Rajnitinama-Madhya Pradesh*; Indra Publishing House Bhopal 2014.
- *Madhya Pradesh Me Zila Sarkar Ki Sthapana per Mukhyamantri Digvijay Singh Ka Sandesh* (CM Message on District Government); Aprils 1999.

- *Madhya Pradesh Sandesh* (MP Govt Publication), November 2011.
- *Press Vigyapatiya* (Official Press Releases of the MP Public Relations Deptt, issued from time to time), Bhopal.
- *Dainik Bhaskar,* Bhopal.
- Girijashankar, *Madhya Pradesh mein Chunavi Rajniti*
- MP Election Booklet on LS election results.

# INDEX

## A

Aam Aadmi Party (AAP) 155
ABVP 7, 9, 14, 18, 43, 155
ADB 7, 4
Advani L K 12, 25, 27, 31, 33, 37, 67, 126,160
Agarwal Lakhiram 12
Agarwal Brij Mohan 19
Agarwal Pramod 62
Agriculture Production Commissioner (APC) 78
Agro–growth 84
Ahluwalia Montek Singh 133
AICC 26, 137, 139, 161, 162, 172
Ajmer Sharif 67
Akriti Group 84
Ali Mushtaq 102
Alirajpur 16
Ambani Anil 39, 126

Anand Marg 9
An Agricultural Testament 73
Andhra Pradesh 16, 20, 74, 115, 120, 125, 129
APC 78, 84
Archaeological Survey of India (ASI) 116
Aron Sunita 24
Arthashastra 103
Arya Samaj 9
Ashok Veer Vikram Singh 114
Ashoka Lake View Hotel 132
Ashoka Road 21, 40
ASSOCHAM 127
Avasya Dr J 124
Ayodhya 25, 26, 35
Azad Ghulam Nabi 177

## B

Babri demolition 18

Bada Malhara 171

Badrinath 67

Bahujan Samaj Party (BSP) 36,
149, 152

Baig Arif 7-9

Bandrabhan 29

Banerjee Mamata 42

Bantadhar Campaign 28, 169

Bastar 16, 147

Basu Jyoti 59

BBC Correspondent 131

BCCI 95

Berwa R N, IAS 149, 152

Begumganj prison 11

Begums of Bhopal 3

Beti Bachao Abhiyan 86

Bhabhara 16

Bhagavad Gita 4, 9

Bhalla Surjit 49

Bhai Ratan Kumar 7

Bhaiyya Raja 114

Bhanpur Babulal 7

Bharti Uma 23-40, 43, 46-47,
109, 132, 140, 153, 158, 160

Bhartiya Jan Shakti (BJS) 35, 38

Bhartiya Janata Yuva Morcha
(BJYM) 11, 21, 30

Bhatt Arun, IAS 126

Bhattacharya AK 64

Bhaya JN 102

Bhind 88

Bhojshala 116

Bhopal Document 149

Bhopal riyasat 3

Bhopal State 3, 31

Bhuria Kantilal 161

Bihar 6, 12, 17, 22, 26, 31, 41,
67, 118, 129, 132, 134, 135,
148, 150

Bijawar 114, 171

BIMARU 71, 80, 96, 118,
122-134, 174

Birbal, IAS 108

Birla Kumar Mangalam 126

Bollywood 105

Bose Ashish 119, 136,

BSP–Bijli–Sadak–Pani 144

Buch MN 148

Budni 11, 14-17, 41

Bundelkhand 23, 26, 47, 114,
150, 170

Business Standard 64, 147

Businessline 144

# C

CG (Chhattisgarh) 19, 49, 125,
129, 133, 134, 143, 146, 147

Chachoda 170

Chanakya 103

Chandidas R 167

Charkhari 23, 24

Chattarpur 114, 170

*Index* 191

Chaturvedi Satyavrat 26, 161, 162
Chouhan Prem Singh 1
Chouhan Shivraj Singh 2, 3, 75, 160, 167, 174, 176
Chautala Abhay 94
Chaudhary Sanjay, IPS 62, 98, 99
Chavan Prithiviraj
Chhatrapati Awards 97
Chhattisgarh 19, 49, 125, 129, 133, 134, 143, 146, 147
Chhindwara 27, 62, 163
Chhindwara Chalak Sangh 62
Chief Ministership 19, 23, 32, 34, 76, 140
Chief Secretary 8, 30, 48, 49, 56, 82, 83, 107-111, 133, 156
Chitale Madhavrao 105
Commonwealth Games scam 59
Communal riots 113
Communist 59
Congress 6-19, 26-28, 31, 36-44, 47, 50, 56, 57, 64, 65, 71, 73, 83, 94, 96, 100-102,118, 122-123, 132, 135, 137-162, 166-173
Correa Charles 143

## D

Dainik Bhaskar 44, 48, 53, 79, 111 142, 170
Dainik Divya Marathi
Dalit Agenda 61, 122, 143, 148-153

Dalits 121, 144, 145, 149-152
Daly College 94, 95
Dantewada 16
Datia 88
Dave Anil 156, 158
Defence Secretary 107
Deputy PM 31
Deputy Speaker 145
Desai Morarji 138
Dasmunshi Priya Ranjan 93
Devi Jamuna 140
Dewas 13, 53, 142
Dhar, near Indore 11
Dhirubhai 126
Dhyanchand Ashok 51, 100
Dikshit Sheila 47
Director General of Police 51, 110
Dube BK, IAS 108
Dumper case 50
Durbar Antar Singh 172

## E

Economic and Political Weekly 70
Eid 52
Emergency 6-13, 137, 152, 168

## F

FAO 69
Firodia Abhay 39, 126
Force Motors 39, 126
Frontline 73

## G

Gadgil Vitthalrao 93
Gadkari Nitin 24, 160, 165
Gandhi Indira 6-10, 14, 71, 138, 177
Gandhi Rajiv 59, 108, 119, 120, 144, 177
Gandhi Sonia 13, 26, 31, 142, 146,
Gaur Babulal 6, 9, 30-33, 37-40, 110-111, 167
Gaur Manoj 50
Gaya 67
Gita Rahasya 10
Global Hunger 123
Godrej Adi 126
Gomatibai 10
Gopalkrishnan R 65
Gopichand P 100
Government School, Shivaji Nagar 4
Governor, Bhai Mahavir 143
Governor of Punjab 108
Green Revolution 69, 71, 135
Gujarati School 4
Gujarat 80, 81, 125, 126, 129, 161
Gupta Narayan 11
Gupta Rajendra 39
Gwalior Chambal 88
Gwalior royal family 95
Gyaneshwar, Sant 10

## H

Haiti 70
Hamidullah 3, 4
Hamidia college 14, 122
Hardia Mahendra 117
Harihar Swarup 65
Haryana 75, 96, 105, 125, 129
Hazare Anna 104
Head Count 119
High Court 43, 102, 107, 110,
Higher Education 53, 87,
Hindu 'hriday samrat' 39
Hindu–Muslim 116
Hindustan Times 29, 40, 81, 110, 123, 139, 146, 148, 169
Holkar 73, 74, 95, 102, 128
Holkar Maharaj 74
Hotel Jehanuma Palace 118
Hoshangabad, district 3, 50, 85
Howard Albert, sir 73
Hubli (Karnataka) 32
HUDCO 116
Hyderabad 3

## I

IAASTD 70
ICD Scam 109, 143
ICS 107
IMR 45, 123, 124, 125
India Today 31, 54, 75, 77, 160
Indian Olympic Association

(IOA) 93
Indian Science Congress 73
India State Hunger Index 123
Indo American Knowledge
Initiative on Agriculture 72
Indore 11, 13, 18, 33, 26, 45, 54, 55, 56, 67, 73, 74, 75, 80, 93-102, 107, 112, 113, 116, 117, 123
Indore Process 73, 74
Industrial disaster, Bhopal 113
Institute of Plant Industry 73, 74
International Fund
for Agro Development 74

# J

Jabalpur 67, 84, 94, 98
Jagathpathy G, IAS 108
Jagdale MM 102
Jahan Sultana 3
Jain Meghraj 11, 15
Jait 1-4, 10, 14
Jaitley Arun 30. 34, 35, 93, 160
Jamaat–e–Islami 9
Jan Ashirwad Yatra 158, 160
Jan Sangh 2, 6–14, 42, 138, 167,
Janani Suraksha Yojana (JSY) 124
Janata Party 12, 13, 137, 138, 168
Jan–Jagran Yatra 15
Javad, Neemuch district 16
Jawaharlal Nehru University

(JNU) 119
Jawahar Lal Nehru 176
Jatiya Dr Satya Narayan 7
Javli 158
Jaypee Cement factory 50
Jha Prabhat 160, 163
Jhakhar Balram 37
Jharkhand 125, 129, 135
Jogi Ajit 145
Joshi Arvind, IAS 111, 112
Joshi Kailash 12, 19, 28, 138, 164
Joshi Murli Manohar 25
Joshi Tinoo 106, 111
Junagarh 3
Justice G G Sohoni Commission 143

# K

Kalmadi Suresh 94
Kanmadikar AW 95
Kansotiya JN 151
Kanyakumari 67
Kartikeya 86
Kaushal Gauri Shankar 9, 13
Kautilya 103
Kautilyan state 103
KBK, Districts 134
Kedarnath 67
Kejriwal Arvind 155
Kela Shashank 152
Kelkar Suryakant 9
Khajuraho Lok Sabha 26

Khan Aamir 105
Khandelwal Pyarelal 11
Khandwa 12, 55, 161
Khargone 55
Khemka Ashok 105
Kisan Panchayat 77
Korput–Bolangir–Kalahandi (KBK) 134
Krishi Cabinet (Agriculture Cabinet) 78
Krishi Karman Award 75
Kumar Anath 166
Kumar Indrajeet 151
Kumar Nitish 176
Shinde Sushil Kumar 100, 177
Kumar Yogesh 47
Kunal 86
Kusmariya Dr. Ramkrishna 171

## L

Ladli Laxmi Yojana 87, 89
Lak Daniel 131
Lalu 40, 93, 132
Deshmukh Vilasrao 93, 96
Scindia Madhavrao 93, 94, 100, 139, 140, 141, 143
Pant KC 93, 94
Laxman Bangaru 20, 21, 22
Lokayukta 46, 104, 111, 112, 143
Lokmanya Tilak 10
London museum 116

London Olympic Games 99
Los Angeles Times 144
Louise Tillin 49
Lucknow 17

## M

Madanlal 36, 100
Mahajan Sumitra 12, 18, 34, 164, 165
Maharashtra 35, 67, 74, 75, 80, 87, 96, 97, 99, 105, 115, 118, 122, 125, 129, 131, 155, 158
Mahidpur 170
Maintenance of Internal Security Act (MISA) 7
Malaiya Jayant 46
Malhotra Satish 95
Malhotra Vijay Kumar 93
Maloo Govind 166
Malviya Devendra 157
Mama 16, 88
Mandal commission 170
Mandale Jail/ Prison 10
Mandsaur 131, 161
Manohar Sai, IPS 151
Master Sharif 9
Mathur P R, IPS 49
Meghraj Jain 11, 15
Ms Mencher Joan P 73
Mendola Ramesh, MLA 171
Menon Arvind 156, 158, 166
MiC Gas 113

*Index*   195

Midas Touch  157

Minister Rajendra Shukla  66, 82

Mishra DP  167

Mishra SK, IAS  62, 156

Mizoram  130

MMR  45, 124,

Model School, Bhopal  4-6

Modi Narendra  12, 39, 47, 59, 93, 126, 155, 158, 177

Mohanty SR, IAS  107, 109, 110

Morena  88

MPCA  95, 101

MPSEB  48, 82

Mr Bantadhar  28

Ms Joan  73

Mukhyamantri Teerth Darshan Yojana  63

Mumbai  59, 95, 118, 122

Murthy NR Narayana  128

Muslim State  3

## N

National Democratic Alliance (NDA)  12, 44, 72, 110, 172

Nagpal Durga Shakti  105

Nagpur  43, 92, 139

Nai Duniya, daily  147

Naidu Chandrakant  39, 169

Naidu Venkaiah  27, 30,

Nanded  67

Nandgaonkar Nitin  5

Nandkumar Sai  19

Narayan Jayaprakash  6, 138,

Narmada, River  3, 4, 29, 54-57, 84

Narmada Puram  50

Narmada Valley Development Authority (NVDA)  55

Nasrulla Ganj  16

Nath Kamal 27, 79, 139, 142, 162, 172

National Games  94, 96, 98

National President of BJP  12

National Rural Health Mission (NHRM)  45, 124

Nawab Khan Hamidullah  3,4

Nawab  3, 4

Naxal  98, 147

NCP  95, 105, 118

Netam Arvind  145

Nilekani Nandan  120

Ninth Plan  124, 134

## O

OBC  27, 121, 140, 150, 151, 153

Omkareshwar  55

Odisha  16, 165, 123, 134

Officers Training Camp (OTC) 13

196 *Shivraj Singh, And Rise Of Madhya Pradesh*

## P

Pachauri Suresh 26, 162, 173
Pai Sudha 152, 167
Panchayats 42, 58, 60, 61
Pande Prem Prakash 19
Pandhre Vijay 105
Panna district 114
Parashuram R, IAS 109
Pataudi Mansoor Ali Khan 8
Patel Praful 93
Patel Pralhad 34, 38, 110,
Pateria Shiv Shankar 114
Patwa Sunderlal 11, 12, 15, 17, 18, 38, 109, 137, 164, 173
Pav–Pav wale bhaiyya 16, 17
Pawar Ajit 93
Pawar Sharad 75, 81, 93, 94, 95, 118, 177
Pawar Tukojirao 53, 74
Peer Gate, Old Bhopal 7
Phir Bhajapa, Phir Shivraj 172
Planning Commission 60, 94, 120, 124, 131-136
Pokhran 165
Pradhan Shailendra 38
Prakash Mohan 162, 172
Pramod Mahajan 25, 27, 30, 34,
Prasad Chandrabhan 149
President George Bush 72
President Mukherjee Pranab 75, 81, 141

President Rule's 138
Prime Minister 6, 14, 27, 31, 40, 54, 71, 81, 83, 107, 108, 119, 133, 139, 142, 148, 170
Prof. Bose 119, 112, 131, 134
Pt. Shukla Ravi Shankar 139
Punjab 75, 80, 99, 100, 101, 108, 122, 123, 125, 130
Puri Case 112
Puri Swaraj, IPS 110, 112
PWD (Public works department) 45, 104, 132, 156

## R

Ranchi National Games 96, 98
Raghavji Bhai 14, 15, 41,114
Raghogarh 40, 41, 138, 169, 170
Rahul 59, 160, 162, 172
Rahmat, Manthan 56
Railway Minister 42
Railway Minister Mamata Banerjee 42
Rajan MP, IAS 132
Rajiv Gandhi Missions on Education 144
Rajmata Scindia Vijayaraje 12, 166
Rajora Rajesh, IAS 111
Rajasthan 56, 115, 118-120, 125, 130, 131
Rajya Sabha 26, 34, 42, 51, 114,

137, 141, 142, 146, 158, 162, 170

Ram Janmabhoomi 24-26

Ranji Trophy National Championships 95

Rao Ashok 146

Rao Hari Ranjan, IAS 128, 156,

Rao PV Narasimha 18, 137, 139, 142, 176

Rashtriya Swayamsewak Sangh (RSS) 11

Rau Prabha 146

Rehmat, 'Manthan' 56

Revenue Board 107

Rewa 49, 50, 62, 66, 67, 100

Rewa division 49

Rout SK, IPS 51

Ruia Anshuman 39

Ruia Shashi 39, 126

## S

Sadhvi 25, 26, 30, 34, 38

Sadhvi Bharti Uma 23-40, 43, 46-47, 109, 110, 132, 140, 153, 158, 160

Sagar constituency 142, 159

Sahani Rakesh, IAS 48, 108

Saifia College 14

Saklecha Virendra Kumar 138

Salkanpur, Raisen district 15

Sanghi Ravi Sharan 39

Sanghvi Vir 139, 141

Sansad 162

Sant Jayanti Ravidas 155, 156

Sarang Kailash 12

Sarasanghchalak (Guriji Golwalkar (Madhav Sadashiv Golwalkar) 11

Sarwate Chandu 102

Satna 159

Sathe Vasant 93

Satyamev Jayate 105

Scam, 2–G 59

Scindia Jyotiraditya Madhavrao 93, 95, 101, 155, 162

Skull cap 52, 53,

Setting Sun (doobta suraj) 162

Sethi P C 8

SGSITS 95

Shahdol 49

Shahgang 86

Shakhas 13

Sharma KS 65

Sharma Lakshmi Kant 112

Sharma Laxmi Narayan 7, 9

Sharma Prasanna 155

Sharma Pratap Bhanu 17

Sharma Raghunandan 36, 38

Sharma Shankar Dayal 31

Sharma Dr Yogiraj 45

Shastri Lal Bahadur 107, 176, 177

Shiva Sena 26
Shivaji Maharaj 158
Shivpuri 43
Shravanbelagola 67
Shreeman Bantadhar 31
Shrivastava Manoj, IAS 62, 67, 122, 156
Shrivastava MK 5
Shrivastava Shailendra, IPS 38, 98, 101
Shripad Dharmadhikary 56
Shukla Chotu 171, 172
Shukla Vidya Charan 94
Shukla Rajendra, Energy Minister 66, 82
Shukla Rajiv 93
Shukla Ravi Shankar 139
Shukla SC 139, 141
Shukla Shyama Charan 139
Shyamla Hills, Bhopal 33, 92, 139, 140, 156
Siddharth 28
Singh Ajay 162
Singh Akhand Pratap 36
Singh Amar 141, 149, 152
Singh Arjun 14, 16, 17, 139, 140, 141 ,143, 145, 146
Singh Asha Rani 114
Singh AV, IAS 65, 30
Singh Bhupendra 62
Singh Chain 2

Singh Digvijay 19, 27, 28, 31, 45, 54, 61, 63, 64, 65, 95, 105, 110, 121, 122, 123, 131, 132, 137, 138, 139, 140, 141, 142, 144, 145, 146, 148, 149, 151, 152, 153, 158, 161, 162, 169, 170, 171, 172
Singh Giani Zail 99
Singh Hari 17
Singh Dr Manmohan 31, 54, 72, 83, 110, 133
Singh Jaiwardhan, MLA 170
Singh Jaswant 37, 62
Singh K K, IAS 45
Singh Laxman 151
Singh LP 107
Singh Mulayam 176
Singh Natwar 93
Singh NK 135
Singh Rajnath 23, 14, 34, 39, 45, 160
Singh Raman 39
Singh RN 107
Singh Sajjan 142
Singh Shivkumar 12
Singh Vibhishan 13
Singh Vijay, IAS 19
Singh Yadvendra 36
Singhdeo KP 94
Singrauli 126
Sisodiya Vijayendra Singh 16
Solanki Shiv Bhanu Singh 140

Soni Hemant 84
Soni Nathuram 8
Soni Sudhir 80
Special Police Establishment (SPE) 112
Special Task Force (STF) 112
Sports Authority of India (SAI) 97, 99
Stern Nicholas 135
Suleman Md, IAS 81
Sunday Express 64
Superintendent of Police 113
Surajkund AICC session 139
Suryavanshi Dilip 40
Swami Lodhi 28, 32
Swaraj Sushma 27, 42, 109, 126, 160
Swarna Jayanti Yatra 27
Swarnim Madhya Pradesh 44
Symbiosis Institute, Pune 39

# T

Tendulkar Sachin 51
Teerth Darshan Yojana 63
Thackeray Balasaheb 26
Thakre Kushabhau 11, 20, 27
Thakkar Himanshu 56
Tikamgarh 26, 36
Time, Magazine 54
Tiwari Arun, IAS 49
Tiwari Congress 143
Tomar Narendra Singh 19, 47,

156, 161, 165, 168
Tribal Leader 140, 145
Tribal Welfare Ministry 161
Tripathi Ajay 62
Tripathi Dr Padmakar 4
Tripathi Akash, IAS 128

# U

UCIL Chairman 113
Ujjain 35, 36, 42, 55, 56, 57, 67, 160, 170
Union Carbide 113
Union Home Secretary 107
UPA 59, 67, 71, 72, 78, 81, 104, 110, 120
Upadhyay MM, IAS 78
UPA–II 59, 104
Urdhwareshe Amul 83
Usha Devi 95
Uttar Pradesh 17, 23, 24, 36, 119, 125, 130, 163
Uttarakhand 67, 130

# V

Vaish Avni, IAS 82
Vaish Rajnish, IAS 55
Vaishno Devi 67
Vajpayee Atal Bihari 12, 17, 22, 26, 31, 41, 127, 148
Vasant Panchami 116
Vengsarkar Dilip 96

200 *Shivraj Singh, And Rise Of Madhya Pradesh*

Verma Sushil Chandra 8

Verma Vikram 12, 18-19, 40, 42, 163–165

VHP 25

Vibhishanji 7

Vibrant Gujarat 126

Vidya Charan Shukla 94

Vikram Awards 97

Vindhya Pradesh 49

Vishwa Hindu Parishad 25

Vishwamitra 97

Vora Motilal 16, 99, 145

# W

Warren Anderson 113

Women's Policy 89

World Bank 74, 83

World Cup Cricket Championships 92

# Y

Yadav Akhilesh 24, 176

Yadav Subhash 139, 140, 161

Yadav Arun 161